JUST MY TYPE

UNDERSTANDING PERSONALITY PROFILES

MICHAEL J. ROSEN

WITH DANIEL CARLSON

TWENTY-FIRST CENTURY BOOKS / MINNEAPOLIS

Acknowledgment: The publisher would like to thank Steve Carlson, PsyD, Adjunct
Faculty, Psychology Department, Saint Mary's University of Minnesota, for his
expert review of this book.

Twenty-First Century Books
A division of Lerner Publishing Group, Inc.
241 First Avenue North
Minneapolis, MN 55401 USA

For reading levels and more information, look up this title at www.lernerbooks.com.

Main body text set in Adrianna Condensed DemiBold 11/15.
Typeface provided by Chank.

Library of Congress Cataloging-in-Publication Data

Rosen, Michael J., 1954–
———Just my type : understanding personality profiles / by Michael J. Rosen with
    Daniel Carlson.
        pages cm
    Audience: Grade 6 to 12.
    Includes bibliographical references.
        ISBN 978-1-4677-8010-0 (lb : alk. paper) — ISBN 978-1-4677-9579-1 (eBook)
        1. Personality—Juvenile literature. I. Title.
    BF698.R8674 2016
    155.2'8—dc23   2015000900

Manufactured in the United States of America
1 – VP – 12/31/15

PERSONALITY

The word "personality" contains 1,307 other words.

Ripley's Believe It or Not!

At last count,

but surely it has

doubled since that.

Personality is invasive.

Allowed into a plot of language

it is more productive

than zucchini. Anyone

who cultivates personality

had better have neighbors

and imaginative recipes

because you are going to be

begging for relief

from your abundance.

You will come to know

it as a nuisance.

—Kay Ryan, United States Poet Laureate, 2008–2010

INTRODUCTION

me, myself, and i

Which ice cream flavor is your favorite?

a. vanilla

b. chocolate

c. strawberry

d. chocolate chip

e. rainbow sherbet

f. rocky road

g. mint chocolate chip

h. coffee

depending on your answer to the quiz on the facing page, neurologist Alan Hirsch, head of the Smell and Taste Treatment and Research Foundation in Chicago, Illinois, can suggest something about your personality. Are you a vanilla lover? If so, you're colorful, intuitive, and a risk taker. Prefer chocolate? You're flirtatious. Strawberry: introverted. Chocolate chip: generous. Rainbow sherbet: pessimistic. Rocky road: aggressive. Mint chocolate chip: confident, frugal, and argumentative. Coffee: dramatic.

What makes for this connection between flavors and personality? Neuroscientists (scientists who study the brain and nervous system) know that a region of the brain called the limbic system oversees both your food preferences and some aspects of personality, which leads Hirsch to theorize that one can correlate to the other.

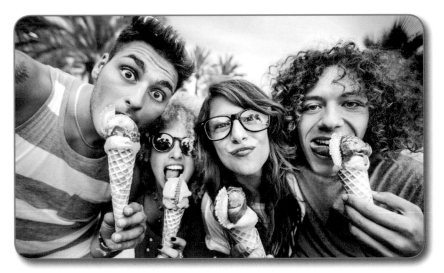

Although other scientists disagree, neurologist Alan Hirsch says that your taste in ice cream (and other foods) says something about your personality. Scientists have been trying to understand human personality since ancient times.

Do you accept Hirsch's theory? If not, you're not alone. Other scientists say that Hirsch's theory about taste and personality is not based on strong scientific research. Although his methods are questionable, Hirsch is hardly alone in trying to understand the workings of human personality. Throughout history, philosophers, scientists, and doctors have tried to do the same thing.

The sciences of psychology and psychiatry emerged in the late nineteenth century. Both psychologists and psychiatrists study the human mind and behavior (although their training is different: psychiatrists attend medical school, while psychologists do not). Psychologists and psychiatrists often use various tests and techniques to assess personality and also to divide people into categories based on personality types.

IN CHARACTER

In ancient times, some doctors believed that the body's fluids, such as blood and phlegm, influenced a person's personality. Other ancient doctors proposed that our exterior appearances matched our interior personalities. They measured and analyzed people's physical characteristics to try to determine their psychological characteristics. Some thinkers looked to the arrangement of stars in the night sky, the bumps on an individual's skull, or handwriting style to understand what made each person tick.

By the nineteenth century, scientists had begun to discuss the unconscious—the thoughts, ideas, and feelings that exist in our minds without us being aware of them. Some psychiatrists tried to find the keys to personality by examining our unconscious behavior.

In the twenty-first century, neuroscientists look for the clues about personality within the brain itself. They use sophisticated tools and techniques such as the electroencephalograph (EEG), an instrument that measures the brain's electrical activity, and positron emission tomography (PET), used to create 3-D images of the brain and other body tissues. Neuroscientists also analyze chemical substances in the body—such as the neurotransmitters that carry nerve impulses and the hormones that help regulate many body functions—to understand human behavior and personality.

WHAT MAKES YOU TICK?

What exactly is personality? According to most twenty-first-century psychologists, it is the set of behavioral and emotional characteristics that makes each individual unique. Personality typing is the attempt to place people who are similar to one another into categories, so that they

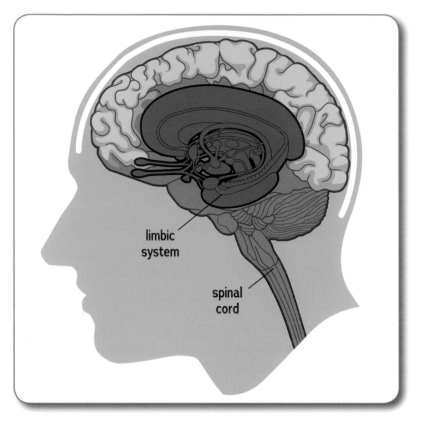

limbic
system

spinal
cord

Some modern scientists study the brain itself to understand personality. A section of the brain called the limbic system plays a large part in determining our traits and emotions.

and others can better understand their moods, actions, and approach to life. Some of this typing is based on rigorous science, while other methods are based on pseudoscience, or beliefs and practices that are mistakenly regarded as scientific.

Isabel Myers, who in 1942 cocreated the Myers-Briggs Type Indicator, a widely used personality test, extolled the benefits of such testing. In the mid-twentieth century, she said, "Whatever the circumstance of your life, the understanding of type can make your perceptions clearer, your judgments sounder, and your life closer to your heart's desire."

Personality testing is big business. Before hiring employees, many businesses use personality tests to gauge how job seekers might perform in

a certain job and how well they might fit into the culture of the organization. Annually, US businesses spend more than $500 million to analyze job seekers through personality tests, and that figure is forecasted to hit $600 million by 2016. Many other organizations—including the military, schools, prisons, and sports teams—also use personality testing to learn more about the people in their ranks. Such information can help leaders anticipate and prevent problems among team members, as well as organize the group for the most efficiency and productivity. Many dating websites use personality quizzes to determine which romantic partners will have the highest chance of a successful pairing.

Testing has its dark sides, however. It can lead to the labeling of certain character traits as deviant, or abnormal. People categorized as deviant risk being victims of harassment, discrimination, or unfair punishment. For instance, up until 1973, US psychiatrists labeled homosexuality a deviant behavior. And throughout the twentieth century, same-sex sexual activity was illegal in many states. Many gay and lesbian people were jailed, committed to mental hospitals, or fired from their jobs because of their so-called deviant behavior. Even in the twenty-first century, personality testing can be used to discriminate against those who don't conform to typical standards of behavior. For instance, even though critics say that workplace personality tests are not a proven gauge of whether someone is suited for a particular job, job seekers can be dropped from consideration for hiring based on personality test results the employer views as undesirable.

THE LIGHTER SIDE

Many types of personality profiling have emerged from serious study. Psychologists have developed them using well-respected theories, verifiable statistical methods, and studies carried out on large sample populations. Some profiling methods are less scientific but can be useful if they help people better understand themselves. Still other personality tests are made simply for fun and entertainment. They are generally written by amateurs, with no scientific training and with no expectation of scientific or therapeutic application. You can find thousands of these amateur tests in magazines and

online. They allow people to determine, for example, their "cuddlability rating"; which Muppet, mixed-martial-arts fighter, or mythological Japanese demon they most resemble; which hot celebrity they will marry; or how likely they are to become one of the richest people in the world. The dating site OkCupid posts links to thousands of online personality tests, and more are launched every day.

The *Toronto Globe and Mail* once observed, "No country in the world is so driven by personality as [the United States]." With social media inviting Americans to express themselves through a wide range of options—from selfies to thumbs-up to emoticons—the statement is truer than ever before. Let's discover why we are so fascinated with personality profiling—and how to smartly assess the reliability and usefulness of the many available tests.

ONE
ORIGINAL thinking

do you know your astrological sign? Does it help you make decisions? Do you believe that the success of worldly affairs and relationships can be found in the heavens? Astrology, the belief that the positions of stars, planets, the sun, and the moon can affect life and events on Earth, dates to ancient times—and it has continued into modern times.

The first people to practice astrology were the Babylonians, who lived in an area that would become modern-day Iraq. They developed a system of astrology as early as 3000 BCE. The ancient Chinese also practiced a form of astrology. It too dates to about 3000 BCE and is based on the positions and movements of

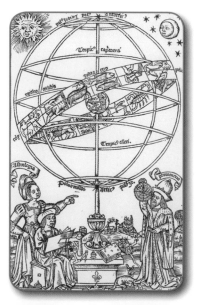

Ptolemy, who lived in the second century CE, was a scholar of geography, mathematics, and astronomy (the study of the universe and the objects in it). He also believed in astrology, the idea that heavenly bodies can influence life and events on Earth. This European woodcut from 1521 shows Ptolemy *(right)* studying stars and planets with a device called an astrolabe.

heavenly bodies. The geographer and mathematician Claudius Ptolemy lived in ancient Alexandria, Egypt. In the second century of the common era (CE), he wrote about astrology in a book called the *Tetrabiblos*. In one passage, he discussed the effects of certain stars on the weather: "The sign of Capricorn [a group of stars] as a whole is moist; but, taken part by part, its leading portion is marked by hot weather and is destructive, its middle temperate, and its following part raises rain-storms. Its northern and southern portions are wet and destructive."

bIRTHDAY GRAB

A traditional Asian way of determining personality, the birthday grab dates back at least one thousand years, to the era of the Song dynasty (ruling family) in China (960–1279). In Chinese the tradition is called *zhua zhou*, which means "pick up" and "first anniversary."

Here's how it works: On a child's first birthday, parents place the baby on a table set with various objects, including foods, tools, toys, books, and weapons. The child crawls toward and picks up whatever object he or she prefers. Whatever the baby grabs is said to indicate his or her future personality and path in life. Historically, some predictions were obvious: Picking a sword suggested that a child would be a warrior. The choice of an abacus suggested a future as a clerk. Other predictions—such as a celery stalk signifying a hard worker, scallions meaning intelligence, or an orange signaling good fortune—were based in Chinese culture and folklore.

The birthday grab is still practiced in several Asian countries, including South Korea and China. As you might guess, some tools of old have been replaced by newer items, such as stethoscopes and calculators. It's not hard to guess what type of future work those items might signify.

For thousands of years, government leaders, scholars, and other prominent people viewed astrology as a reliable science. Early astrologers created horoscopes—complex diagrams showing the position of astral bodies (typically the sun, moon, and planets) at a certain time, such as the moment of someone's birth. Astrologers used these diagrams to predict important events, such as the birth of kings and victories in battle. Ancient astrologers also used horoscopes to forecast human destinies. For instance, an astrologer might note a strong influence of the planet Mars—named for the ancient Roman god of war—at the time a baby was born and from this predict that the child would be redheaded, athletic, ambitious, and assertive.

HUMOROLOGY: NOTHING FUNNY ABOUT IT

Humorology was an early medical concept developed by Hippocrates, a Greek physician who lived around 400 BCE. He theorized that good health required a balancing of four body fluids: blood, yellow bile (a liquid that digests fats in the liver and colon), black bile (a liquid then believed to be secreted by the kidneys or spleen), and phlegm. Hippocrates said that if an individual possessed too much or too little of one fluid, he or she would be physically sick. He also said that each fluid was connected to a certain temperament, or mood.

TRY IT

If you suffered from anger-management problems in ancient Greece, what would the leading physician diagnose?

1. Your brain chemistry is out of sync with your body. Seek the advice of a healer at one of the temples of the god Apollo.

2. Such problems run in your family. Most likely, the anger is an affliction caused by your ancestors' sins. Live with your fate.

3. You suffer from an imbalance of your body's fluids. Change your diet: eat more leafy vegetables, citrus fruits, and herbs such as rosemary and sage.

4. Such rage! Such power! Join the army!

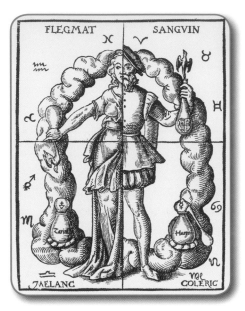

This illustration from *Quinta Essentia*, a 1574 book by Swiss physician Leonhard Thurneysser, shows four individuals—each with a different dominant humor—blended into one body. First proposed by Hippocrates in ancient Greece, the concept of the four humors—which were said to account for both health and personality—influenced physicians into the eighteenth century.

The physician Claudius Galenus, or Galen, who lived in the Roman Empire in the second century CE, expanded the concept of the four humors. He identified four distinct personality types, each one connected with one of the four humors. Someone's personality, Galen said, depended on which humor was dominant in his or her body. Those who were heavy on blood were called sanguine. They were said to be extroverted, people-oriented, flighty, and emotional. Those who were heavy on yellow bile were said to be choleric. That made them independent, decisive, firm, and hot-tempered, with bottled-up emotions. Phlegm-heavy people were described as phlegmatic—which meant they were friendly, pragmatic, and uncomfortable with change. Those dominated by black bile were thought to be melancholic. They were thought to be logical, reserved, detail-oriented, detached, and high-strung.

Galen and other doctors believed that the body's fluids could be brought into balance by a change in diet. So, based on this belief, the correct answer to the boxed quiz on the opposite page is number 3: Your anger-management problems are likely caused by an excess of yellow bile. You need to cool your hot temper with foods such as cucumbers, melons, dandelion greens, and lime juice. (In later centuries, doctors also used bloodletting—or draining a patient's blood—to try to balance the humors.)

CIVIL SERVICE

1. Briefly describe those situations in which it is appropriate to conduct an infantry charge against a larger enemy force.
2. Compose a poem in the classical style on the theme of the fleeting nature of life.
3. Outline the process by which land is prepared for the planting, growing, and harvesting of rice.

In ancient China, between about 200 BCE and 200 CE, people who wanted jobs with the government had to demonstrate their intelligence by answering test questions such as these. They had to show knowledge of military affairs, law, agriculture, economics, geography, and the writings of the Chinese philosopher Confucius—all subjects deemed crucial to proper governance.

This practice shows that one of the first mental traits that humankind sought to measure was smarts. But intelligence is just one aspect of personality. And being smart doesn't mean that someone is well suited for a particular job or challenge. Other traits, such as empathy, friendliness, manual dexterity, or an ability to organize well might be just as important.

In the twenty-first century, schools and other organizations still rely heavily on intelligence tests to judge the likelihood of success or failure, even though modern research shows that the tests are imperfect indicators. Again, other qualities, such as problem-solving skills, confidence, and previous experience, contribute just as much to success as intelligence does—sometimes even more.

ABOUT FACE

Another ancient method for assessing personality was physiognomy, the idea that someone's facial and other physical features revealed his or her character. In ancient China, a physiognomy practice called Mien Shiang recognized eleven distinctive facial shapes. These shapes were linked to the five basic elements of the universe recognized by Chinese philosophy: wood, earth, fire, water, and metal. According to Mien Shiang, a strong brow and a boxy face were linked to wood and were signs of leadership and passion. Those with full mouths and chins, fleshy cheeks, and fleshy earlobes were connected to earth and were said to be empathic and nurturing. Fire was shown in an oval face with bright eyes and a brilliant smile, which revealed that the person was spontaneous and magnetic. Those who sought wisdom and truth were connected to water. They had full cheeks, dreamy eyes, and square-set jaws. Finally, those with high eyebrows, angular cheekbones, and slender noses were linked to metal and were thought to be organized and charitable.

In the West, the practice of physiognomy dates to the sixth century BCE in ancient Greece. Then people believed that an individual's physical and mental characteristics were one and the same. So they thought that you *could* judge a book by its cover. Adherents of physiognomy in ancient Greece believed that especially long ears signaled a fool and that witty, thrifty, and modest individuals possessed small and thin ears. Wide nostrils on a man denoted a lustful nature. Eyebrows close together were signs of a dull but good friend. Eyebrows far apart meant that someone was hard-hearted, vain, and greedy. The ancient Greeks also assigned personality attributes based on hair color, thickness, and degree of curliness.

One subset of ancient physiognomy involved comparing individuals to the animals they most resembled. Someone with the physical attributes of a bull (a thick and wide head), for instance, would be considered unintelligent but physically powerful. Someone with elongated facial features, resembling those of a horse, was thought to possess that beast's regal and spirited nature.

Such judgments influenced Western society for more than two thousand years, creating assumptions about what a good, bad, moral, or immoral

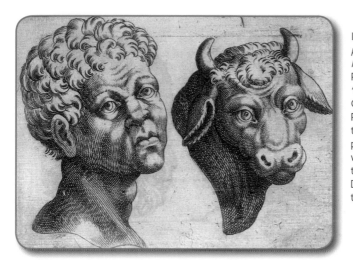

In his *De humana physiognomonia libri* (Book of Human Physiognomy) from 1586, Italian scholar Giambattista della Porta asserted that people share personality traits with the animals they resemble. Della Porta likened this man to a bull.

individual looked like. In his book *Christian Morals,* seventeenth-century British physician and philosopher Thomas Browne wrote, "Since the Brow speaks often true, since Eyes and Noses have Tongues, and the countenance [facial expression] proclaims the heart and inclinations; let observation so far instruct thee in Physiognomical lines." So Browne believed that you could judge someone just by examining his or her face.

A BUMP ON THE HEAD

As the centuries passed, scientists learned more about the workings of the human body. During the Middle Ages (about 500 to 1500 CE), doctors in the Middle East and Europe began exploring human anatomy and body systems. Science leaped forward as scholars began to emphasize natural explanations over supernatural ones. They relied upon observation, evidence, and measurements to learn about the world around them. In the eighteenth century, some European doctors hired grave robbers to bring them dead bodies. The doctors would then dissect and examine the corpses to learn more about the workings of the human body.

Not all new medical theories were sound, however. For instance, in the eighteenth and nineteenth centuries, a German scientist named Franz Josef Gall studied the human brain. He devised a practice called phrenology, based on the idea that the size and placement of a bump or depression on

someone's skull directly corresponded to the workings of the part of the brain beneath that particular spot. He identified twenty-seven distinct "cerebral organs" within the brain, each possessing its own function. The *Farbensinn* region was said to be associated with "a disposition for colouring, and the delighting in colours." The *Dichtergeist* region was connected with "poetic talent." An area called *Kunstsinn* controlled "mechanical skill," and *Jungenliebe* was linked to "tenderness for the offspring." Gall and other phrenologists believed that people could retrain or encourage any given spot in the brain with specific mental exercises.

Phrenology became popular in the United States in the early nineteenth century. Phrenologists opened clinics and wrote pamphlets and how-to manuals for aspiring practitioners. Some employers gave phrenology exams to job applicants to try to gauge their trustworthiness. Some couples took phrenology exams to find out if they would be compatible spouses. In her 1848 book *Familiar Lessons on Physiology*, Lydia Fowler directed families to use phrenology "as a pilot to enable children to avoid the shoals [sandbars] and quicksands of life."

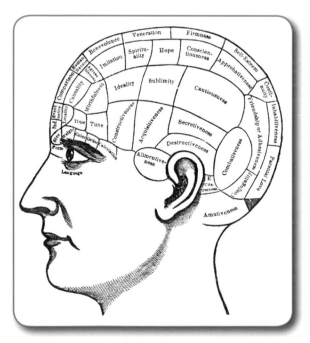

According to phrenologists, bumps on the skull revealed what was happening inside the brain. This engraving from the 1875 book *The Phrenological Journal and Life Illustrated*, by Samuel Wells, provides a detailed map of the skull and personality traits said to be associated with each region.

THE PEN CAN'T LIE

Graphology, or handwriting analysis, involves studying how people cross their *t*'s and dot their *i*'s—and almost every other aspect of penmanship—to glean information about personality. Some historians say that the science dates to 500 BCE in China, but the first known practitioner of graphology was the philosopher Aristotle in ancient Greece. In a text dating to 330 BCE, he wrote, "Speech is the expression of ideas or thoughts or desires. Handwriting is the visible form of speech. Just as speech can [express] emotions, somewhere in handwriting is an expression of the emotions underlying the writer's thoughts, ideas, or desires."

More than two thousand years later, Jean-Hippolyte Michon, a French clergyman and archaeologist, revived Aristotle's idea. He founded the Society of Graphology in Paris, France, in 1871. He argued that a person's penmanship possessed "fixed signs" that revealed character. He also believed that handwriting flowed spontaneously from the unconscious and was thus a form of "soulwriting." Michon claimed, for example, that thick letters written with great firmness indicated sensuality, whereas airy writing was a sign of modesty. Cheerful people opened up their letters just as "laughter parts the lips," he wrote. Their letters were plump and never condensed. Their *t*'s were crossed with curving, delicate bars.

CRIMINAL COURT

In Europe and the United States, people continued to use physiognomy to evaluate personality. Some people believed that you could spot criminal tendencies in a person's face. In his book *Criminal Man,* published in 1876, Italian criminologist Cesare Lombroso stated that the "born criminal" could be identified through features such as a large jaw, handle-shaped ears, fleshy lips, a pointy head, or a meager beard. The invention of photography in the mid-nineteenth century added momentum to the era's enthusiasm for physiognomy. Criminologists and scientists studied and compared photos of individuals, looking for specific traits that pointed to criminal tendencies.

In the mid-twentieth century, scientists at Harvard University near Boston, Massachusetts, also proposed that criminals could be identified by their physical traits. After World War II (1939–1945), the German physician

Oskar Vogt requested permission to examine the brains of German officers who had been executed for war crimes, namely the systematic murder of six million Jews and other Europeans during the war. Vogt hoped that his brain studies of these murderers and torturers would reveal an explanation for the atrocities. The officials in charge of the war crimes trials denied his requests.

The practice of identifying criminals based on appearance has continued as racial profiling. For instance, studies and statistics show that US police tend to stop and search people with dark skin, such as African Americans, more often than they apprehend people with light skin. This practice—which violates protections provided by the US Constitution—is based on the false assumption that dark-skinned people are more likely to be involved with criminal behavior.

mind and matter

during the seventeenth century, as scientists were beginning to uncover the secrets of the human body, French philosopher René Descartes developed the concept of mind-body dualism. He observed that the mind and body operate together but that each entity has certain powers and certain limits. For instance, the mind can control movements of the arms and legs, but it cannot stop the ears from hearing or the gums from extruding a wisdom tooth. The body, meanwhile, can provide data to the mind—such as sensations we feel with our skin or images we see with our eyes, but the body cannot think. Descartes identified the brain as the location of the mind and of thought.

In the following centuries, doctors continued to study the human body and also the workings of the mind. German doctor Wilhelm Wundt founded the first psychological laboratory, in the German city of Leipzig, in 1879. To learn about the workings of the human brain, he focused on the observation of human behavior. Specifically, Wundt measured how quickly subjects responded to a sound or a light. He theorized that someone who reacted to an event quickly was also thinking faster than other people.

British scientist Francis Galton, who worked in the late nineteenth century, helped set the groundwork for modern psychological study. Previously, when researchers sought evidence about the mind or body, they

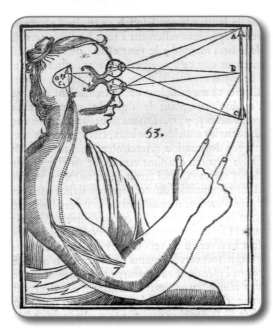

French philosopher René Descartes put forth the idea of mind-body dualism. He noted how the mind and body work together as well as separately. This engraving, which illustrates Descartes's idea, comes from his *De Homine* (On Man), published in 1662, twelve years after his death.

focused long and hard on a single individual and collected volumes of data on that one person. Galton's approach was different. He undertook more limited research on a wider selection of test takers. For example, he offered money to poor people to come to his London laboratory and allow him to record such data as height, finger length, and lung capacity. This approach gave Galton an understanding of average physical traits to be found in a large group of people. He then looked for deviations—longer fingers, for instance, or shallower breathing—that might be connected to particular psychological traits.

Galton also pioneered the investigation of whether nature (inherited factors) or nurture (environmental influences) shapes personality. He wondered if personality is inherited from one's parents (nature) or is developed and changed over time by a person's surroundings (nurture). In the nurture theory of personality, a child's cruelty could be explained by that person having consistently observed cruelty. A friendly child would have close friendships, and so on. Those who support the nature theory believe that personality traits are inherited and are fixed from birth. By the twenty-first century, most scientists believe that a combination of nature and nurture determines human personality.

Galton also laid the groundwork for the concept of correlation: that is, the extent to which two factors are causally related. For example, he attempted to assess the relationship between heredity and genius. He asked: Is a child's intelligence determined by the intelligence of the child's parents? But rather than applying math or biological science to his question, he used only anecdotal evidence—that is, stories, observations, and biographical information. Based on the assumption that intelligence was linked to professional success, Galton studied only prominent men, such as British war

two heads are better

One way modern psychologists explore the nature-versus-nurture question is by studying twins: two children created in the same pregnancy. Identical twins (who develop from one fertilized egg that splits to form two embryos) have exactly the same genes—the chemical markers, passed down from parents to their children that determine a person's physical traits. Because identical twins share the same genes, researchers can assume that their nature is similar and that any differences in traits or behaviors can be explained by nurture—the different experiences the twins have while growing up.

Research since the late nineteenth century—beginning with Francis Galton in 1875—has shown that identical twins, even those raised separately, tend to have similar personalities, interests, intelligence quotients (IQs), and attitudes. One extensive study, the Minnesota Twin Family Study, followed the experiences and behavior of twins for twenty years in the late twentieth century. As psychologist and science writer Scott Barry Kaufman relates, the study found that "identical twins reared apart were eerily similar to identical twins reared together on various measures of personality, occupational and leisure-time interests, and social attitudes."

heroes and members of Parliament. His findings, gathered in his 1869 book *Hereditary Genius*, argue that yes, children do inherit intelligence from their parents. But Galton failed to factor in the influence of environment, including a family's ability to provide for its offspring's health, nutrition, and education. In this case, the men he studied all came from privileged backgrounds, which had helped them succeed professionally. Because Galton didn't look at environment, he assumed that success equals intelligence and based his findings on only anecdotal evidence. Most scholars discredit his study.

Identical twins Tamara Rabi and Adriana Scott demonstrate this point. Born in Mexico and adopted as babies, they were raised by different families in the United States—Adriana on Long Island, New York, and Tamara in New York City. In 2003, when they were reunited at the age of twenty, they discovered that they had much in common: both were B students, and both called themselves "night people." They both said they wanted to have children—a boy and girl, in that order. They both used Pantene shampoo, and their favorite movie was the same: *A League of Their Own*. But the twins were also different in some ways, since they had had different life experiences. Stories like this, as well as the Minnesota Twin Family Study and others, show that nature accounts for a great deal of our personality traits, with nurture also contributing.

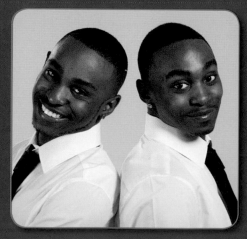

Identical twins—even those who do not grow up together—often have quite similar personalities. Scientists attribute these similarities to genetics, since identical twins have the exact same genes.

UNDER THE SKIN

A giant in the field was Austrian physician Sigmund Freud. Working in the late nineteenth century and early twentieth century, he examined René Descartes's ideas about the mind and the body and developed them further. Freud said that certain body reactions are governed by the unconscious mind—the part of the brain over which we have no control. For instance, someone might feel frightened by a sudden noise at night or feel hungry when smelling a favorite food. The person can't control these reactions—they are determined in the unconscious mind.

Freud believed that the unconscious mind motivates most human behavior. He said that unconscious motivations lie beneath the surface of our thoughts, projecting themselves—without our conscious permission or even our knowledge—onto our actions, reactions, and dreams. According to Freud, the unconscious mind contains repressed memories, fears, sexual longings, and secrets, which emerge on their own, taking the form of fear, wrath, pride, envy, lust, and other challenging emotions. He explained, "No mortal can keep a secret. If his lips are silent, he chatters with his fingertips; betrayal oozes out of him at every pore."

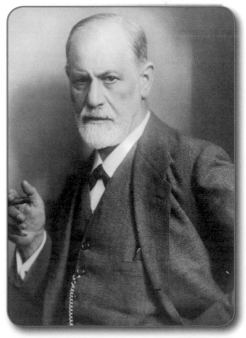

Freud developed psychoanalysis, a form of talk therapy through which patients examine their unconscious minds and bring their troubling emotions and experiences to the forefront. In this process, the patient expresses his or her thoughts in response to prompts from the analyst.

Austrian physician Sigmund Freud developed the process of psychoanalysis in the late nineteenth century. Using this technique, an analyst tries to uncover the fears, fantasies, secrets, and longings within a patient's unconscious mind.

By asking about dreams, fears, and fantasies, an analyst coaxes the analysand's (patient's) unconscious to reveal inner conflicts. Then the analyst interprets these problems and works with the patient to address and resolve them. The idea is that by consciously confronting negative emotions, a patient can strip those emotions of their power and achieve a healthier, more peaceful mental state.

Psychologist Alfred Adler, a colleague of Freud's in Vienna, was less focused on the unconscious. In his studies, he looked at the individual as a whole—including the person's family dynamics, friendships, home environment, and work life—to understand human behavior. Adler also believed that the conscious and the unconscious worked together to frame personality and behavior.

"THE PASSWORD IS . . ."

Personality assessments known as word association tests were first developed by Swiss psychiatrist Carl Jung, working in the early twentieth century. Sigmund Freud described the unconscious as inherently chaotic and amoral—something that needed to be confronted and corrected. Jung, in contrast, saw the unconscious as a neutral entity that did not necessarily require curing. He used word association tests to gather information about patients' minds—not to try to fix them. Try the word association test below.

TRY IT

Read each word on the list below. After each word, immediately say the first thing that comes to your mind. This is an example of word association.

Safety	Protection
Children	Money
Woman	Power
Weakness	Danger
Adult	Man

Jung proposed that the unconscious mind hid in the background of the conscious mind to coach its behaviors. To reach the unconscious, Jung said, one need only provide some stimulus, such as a prompting word. The first thing that popped into the test taker's mind—compliments of the unconscious—would reveal how that individual made associations or connections. For example, let's say the first word that came into your head in response to the word *protection* was the word *condom.* A psychiatrist like Jung might wonder if this response means that you are a hypersexual person. Or does the response suggest that you are fearful of sexual encounters? If many or all of your responses to the words related to sexual behavior, a psychiatrist might want to further discuss sexual issues with you.

SEEING THINGS: RORSCHACH TESTS

Word association tests are called projective tests because they require that test takers project—or cast—their interior feelings or thoughts onto exterior objects, words, or images. The Rorschach test is another kind of projective test.

In the early twentieth century, Swiss psychiatrist Hermann Rorschach developed clusters of inkblots, presented on individual cards, which he used as a tool to diagnose schizophrenia—a brain disorder characterized by delusions, hallucinations, and other kinds of extremely disturbed thinking and behavior. As it turned out, the test could not diagnose schizophrenia, so psychiatrists began using it instead to learn about the mind as a whole. They showed test takers ten consecutive cards—five with black inkblots and five with colored inkblots—and asked them what each image brought to mind. The examiner looked for patterns or themes that emerged in the test taker's responses to the ten images and also noted what responses strayed from the typical responses provided by other test takers.

Psychiatrists and law enforcement agencies continued to use the Rorschach test throughout the twentieth century and into the twenty-first. But some professionals say that the Rorschach and other projective tests provide no valid information. Scientists have found little data to link certain test responses to certain conditions, traits, or behaviors. That's because everyone's worldview is different. We all have different upbringings and

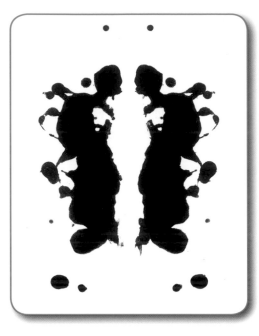

Psychiatrists have used the Rorschach test since the early twentieth century. Created by Swiss doctor Hermann Rorschach, the test involves a series of cards like this one. Test takers say what the images bring to mind. The responses are meant to give insights into a test taker's behavior and personality.

cultural values, which lead to diverse reactions to projective test questions. It's difficult to determine what a "normal" response to a question is when everyone gives a different answer. Another drawback with projective tests is that test takers don't always tell the truth about what a word, shape, or image reminds them of.

Some critics even describe the Rorschach and other projective tests as pseudoscience. Psychologist Arthur S. Reber wrote in 1985, "An intense dialogue [between a doctor and patient] about the wallpaper or the rug would do as well [as a Rorschach test]." Reber believed that the inkblots could be a good tool for jump-starting a therapy session but that they offered no special scientific insight into a patient's mind.

RAT-A-TAT-*TAT*

In the early twentieth century, as psychiatrists and psychologists learned more about the brain and personality, large organizations became interested in assessing the competence and character of individuals who sought to join their ranks. One of these organizations was the US Army. In the 1930s, the army hired psychologists to create the Thematic Apperception Test (TAT).

Like the Rorschach test, the TAT had test takers respond to images, but it used realistic pictures instead of abstract inkblots. One TAT card showed a picture of a farm, a horse, a man working, a young woman with books, and an older woman. Test takers were asked to describe what they thought was going on in the picture. Trained interpreters would analyze the test taker's responses to this picture and those on other TAT cards to determine the test taker's worldview. An individual's responses would be analyzed on their own or analyzed in comparison to the responses of a large group of other test takers. The idea was to flag those whose responses were atypical. These test takers might be dropped from consideration for a specific army job or assignment or lined up for further testing or interviews.

After the Second World War, clinicians outside the army began to use the TAT to evaluate patients suspected of suffering from emotional problems. The TAT method spread to mainstream society during the 1960s and 1970s. As part of the US counterculture movement of this era—a youth-driven rebellion against established social norms, including organized religion—many Americans sought spiritual fulfillment and a better understanding of their inner selves. Up until then, most people sought psychological or psychiatric guidance only to deal with brain disorders and other mental health issues. Starting in the 1960s, many Americans

Projection booth

Projective tests have made it into popular media. For example, the fictional spy hero James Bond (played by Daniel Craig) takes a word association test in the movie *Skyfall* (2012). In MTV's first episode of *Daria* (1997–2001), the lead character takes a test similar to the TAT. Projective tests are also used in the movies *A Clockwork Orange* (1971) and *Flowers for Algernon* (2000). In short, when screenwriters want to show that a researcher is attempting to find out how a character's mind works, the go-to is the projective test.

TRY IT

Answer yes or no to these four questions from the Woodworth Personal Data Sheet.

1. Can you stand the sight of blood?
2. Do you usually feel well and strong?
3. Do things ever seem to swim or get misty before your eyes?
4. Is it easy to get you cross or grouchy?

consulted with psychologists as part of their quests for fulfillment. Many clinicians used the TAT with those clients.

Look at the questions at the top of this page. These are four of the hundred-plus questions included on the Woodworth Personal Data Sheet, also known as the Woodworth Psychoneurotic Inventory. Robert S. Woodworth of the American Psychological Association developed the test during World War I (1914–1918). The US Army gave the test to potential soldiers to diagnose their likelihood of being susceptible to immobilizing fear or other vulnerabilities due to the stress and trauma of combat. The questions helped the army determine whether a man was emotionally unstable and unfit for military duty.

Woodworth's test was a breakthrough for psychological testing. Unlike projective tests, which require time-intensive, one-on-one analysis by a trained professional, Woodworth's test was easy to score. An examiner simply had to compare a soldier's answers with a sheet of desired answers to determine whether a man was fit for battle. This kind of self-reporting made testing easier and less time-consuming. It influenced and opened the way for other personality tests.

GOOD BEHAVIOR

American psychologist John B. Watson, a professor at Johns Hopkins University in Baltimore, Maryland, founded the behaviorist school of thought in 1913. Unlike Freud and Jung, Watson didn't focus on the unconscious. He believed that a person's internal mental states and preferences were

too difficult to measure, identify, and treat. Watson said that instead of confronting the unconscious, individuals would be better served by minimizing traits or behaviors that caused problems in their lives. Behaviorist science focuses on observable, measurable events, not on mental states. Other well-known behaviorists are Ivan Pavlov and B. F. Skinner.

The primary tenet of behaviorism is that human responses and actions—and to a great extent personality—are learned from childhood. Watson said that you could change human behavior with rewards and punishments, just as you might train a cat to stay off the furniture by using a spray of water or reward a dog for obeying by giving it a liver treat. Watson said that for humans, disincentives to bad behavior include disapproval of peers or parents, or physical punishment in extreme situations. Rewards for good behavior include the praise or acceptance of others.

Actively embracing this concept, Watson claimed that any type of person could be shaped into any other type of person. He stated, "Give me a dozen healthy infants, well-formed, and my own specified world to bring them up in and I'll guarantee to take any one at random and train him to become any type of specialist I might select—doctor, lawyer, artist, merchant-chief and, yes, even beggar-man and thief, regardless of his talents, penchants, tendencies, abilities, vocations, and race of his ancestors."

To prove his theories, Watson carried out various experiments. In one landmark study in 1920, he and a Johns Hopkins graduate student named Rosalie Rayner successfully conditioned a baby named Albert to fear a small rat. The experiment started with the researchers noting Albert's perplexed reactions to a variety of objects and animals, including a handbag, a white rabbit, and a white rat. In this way, they determined that Albert was not afraid of rats. Next, Watson made a loud and frightening noise whenever Rayner showed Albert a white rat. The noise caused Albert to cry. After repeating this activity several times, Watson showed Albert the rat without making the noise. Albert reacted with the same level of fear as he had before. Albert also reacted with fear when he saw a white rabbit, because he had extended his fear to include any small and furry white animal.

Watson's theories influenced the study of the human mind until the 1960s. Modern researchers dismiss his ideas as overly simplistic. They

Only human

A new school of psychological thought emerged in the 1950s. Led by American Abraham Maslow and others, this was the humanist school. Humanist psychologists thought that the Freudians and behaviorists were too focused on the negative aspects of human behavior. They instead emphasized human potential, creativity, and free will—the ability of people to work to improve their emotional lives. A more recent school of thought, positive psychology, is similar. It too focuses on what is right with people instead of what is wrong. Positive psychologists emphasize the role of hope and optimism in improving mental health.

point out that people can change trained behavior by either intentionally or unintentionally learning new behavior. That is, an old dog can learn new tricks.

Despite this criticism, some aspects of behaviorist theories are still used. For instance, twenty-first-century counselors sometimes use positive or negative reinforcement to help people overcome addiction to harmful substances, such as cigarettes.

THAT SMARTS!

The twentieth century also saw the development of the first modern intelligence tests. In 1905 French psychologist Alfred Binet and his student Theodore Simon published an intelligence scale that could help schools identify students who were mentally disabled and needed special assistance. This test, the Binet-Simon Intelligence Scale, did not assess an individual's academic knowledge. Instead, it evaluated a person's ability to reason, process questions, and retain information. The test was designed to give a rough "mental age" of the test taker.

A German psychologist, William Stern, developed the concept of the intelligence quotient, or IQ, in 1912. Stern set the average person's IQ at 100

and then created a formula to determine individual IQs. That formula is (mental age ÷ chronological age) × 100. Suppose that the Binet-Simon test shows that a fifteen-year-old has a mental age of twenty. Plug these numbers into the formula and you get an IQ of 133 ($20 ÷ 15 = 1.33$; $× 100 = 133$).

Robert Yerkes, who studied comparative psychology and animal behavior at Harvard University and became president of the American Psychological Association in 1917, created intelligence tests for the US Army. The tests were supposed to screen out men who were not smart enough to be soldiers. The army gave the test to thousands of recruits during World War I.

Many men who took the tests were recent immigrants to the United States who did not know English well. Not surprisingly, they scored considerably lower than test takers who were born in the United States. But it wasn't just language skills that made the immigrants score poorly. The tests measured acculturation more than intelligence. That is, they measured familiarity with US culture. For instance, one question asked test takers to

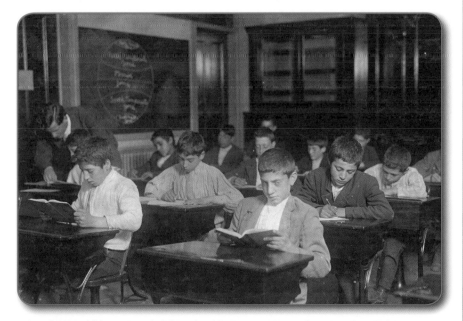

Immigrant children attend night school in Boston, Massachusetts, circa 1909. When they took intelligence tests, immigrants of this era often scored lower than native-born Americans. Critics say that the tests measured an individual's familiarity with US culture more than they measured actual intelligence.

a dumb IDEA

Intelligence testing in the early twentieth century helped fuel the eugenics movement in the United States. Eugenics promotes the idea of "improving" the human race by encouraging people with certain traits to have children while discouraging or actively preventing (through medical sterilization) those with less desirable traits from having children.

After intelligence testing became popular in the United States, eugenicists argued that people with low IQ scores should not be allowed to reproduce. Some took the argument even further, arguing for the forced sterilization of criminals, the homeless, homosexuals, prostitutes, the disabled, the poor, people of color, and others who were seen as undesirable members of society. Many state governments in the United States followed through, arranging for the forced sterilization of tens of thousands of poor and minority individuals. The practice continued in some states until the 1970s.

identify Crisco, a commercial vegetable shortening that was popular in the United States in the early twentieth century. Most native-born Americans of this era would have been familiar with the product, but an immigrant from Russia would have had no idea what it was.

In the twenty-first century, schools, businesses, the military, and other organizations still use IQ testing, although modern tests are more sensitive to cultural differences than were tests of the World War I era. The Binet-Simon Intelligence Scale (renamed the Stanford-Binet Intelligence Scale in the mid-twentieth century) has been updated five times since it was first developed. The most recent update was in 2003.

THREE
trait theory

during the twentieth century, some psychologists abandoned psychoanalytic theory and other methods of assessing personality in favor of an approach called trait theory. Trait theory holds that someone's personality is composed of many unrelated but interacting internal features. Researchers who promote trait theory say that these traits can be measured and compared to explain how individuals are both similar to and different from one another.

TYPE CASTING

The first researcher to suggest that personalities could be typed according to traits was Swiss psychotherapist Carl Jung. In 1921 Jung published a book called *Psychologische Typen (Psychological Types)*. In it he explained that people could be grouped into types determined by their behaviors. Jung established the groups based on three questions.

He asked: Is a person extroverted or introverted? In other words, to what extent does an individual crave stimulation from external sources? As Jung noted, extroverts tend to look for stimulation outside themselves— from friends and social activities, for example. Introverts tend to look for stimulation from within. Jung then asked whether a person was guided more by thinking or by feeling. Thinkers, he said, made decisions based on careful logic. Feelers made decisions on gut reactions.

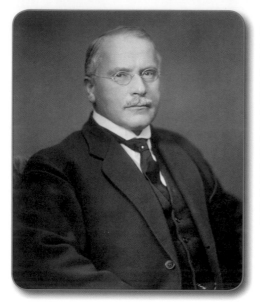

In the early twentieth century, Swiss psychiatrist Carl Jung grouped people according to personality types. For instance, he identified introverts (those who find satisfaction by looking inside themselves) as well as extroverts (those who prefer more social interaction). Jung's introvert-extrovert model remains at the heart of many modern personality-typing systems.

The last question concerned how a person takes in information. Some people use their five senses to gather data. Jung described these people as sensing. Others rely more on hunches, instinct, and previous experience. Jung said that these people were intuitive.

Every person, Jung believed, consciously expressed one side of the spectrum or the other in each of the three categories. He said that the side that wasn't expressed would be revealed through unconscious actions. For instance, if a person's conscious behavior showed him or her to be a thinker, then the person's unconscious actions would reveal his or her feeling side. But Jung also cautioned that it was unwise to try to pigeonhole people into rigid type categories. He wrote, "Every individual is an exception to the rule."

THE FOUR THOUSAND TRAITS OF GORDON ALLPORT

The concept of cardinal, central, and secondary traits comes from US psychologist Gordon Allport, a professor at Harvard University. In the mid-twentieth century, he looked at groups of cardinal, central, and secondary traits—and the extent to which each group governed a person's life—to understand that person's personality. To create a list of traits, Allport looked

through a dictionary and selected more than four thousand words that could be used to describe personality. Like most modern psychologists, Allport believed that these traits derived from nature as well as nurture.

TRY IT

Set a timer for sixty seconds. In that interval, list as many of your personality traits as you can think of.

Once you've made your list, organize the traits based on how much impact they have on your overall character. Does one trait, perhaps your outgoing nature, dominate your personality? If so, this is your cardinal trait. What other traits are key to your personality? Maybe you are witty and empathic. Then wit and empathy would be your central traits. The traits that are not at the core of your personality but that arise under certain conditions—for instance, when you're stressed or preoccupied—are called your secondary traits. An example of those traits might be impatience or aloofness.

In 1946 Raymond Cattell, a British-born psychologist, used Allport's ideas to create a personality test. Cattell examined Allport's list of 4,000-plus traits and noted that many of the words were either synonymous (such as charming and charismatic), closely connected (smart and eloquent), or oppositional (intelligent and unintelligent). He used these connections to narrow down the 4,000-plus traits to 171.

Using an early-model computer, Cattell then subjected his list to the newly developed statistical technique known as factor analysis. This technique shows the extent to which two or more factors—in this case, personality traits—can be reasonably and accurately grouped together. For example, kindness and warmth are closely allied, as are impatience and tenseness. Cattell grouped such like traits together to make fewer and more manageable categories. In this way, he narrowed down the 171 personality traits to just 16 traits: warmth, reason, emotional stability, dominance, liveliness, rule-consciousness, social boldness, sensitivity, vigilance, abstractness, privateness, apprehension, openness to change, self-reliance, perfectionism, and tenseness.

Based on this work, Cattell and a team of international colleagues created the Sixteen Personality Factor (16PF) questionnaire, designed to reveal the traits that most pertain to a given individual. First published in 1949 and revised four times in the late twentieth century, the test consisted of a series of statements. For each statement, respondents gave an answer ranging from 1 to 5, with 1 meaning that the statement was very inaccurate and with 5 meaning that the statement was very accurate. Here are a few examples:

1. I suspect hidden motives in others.
2. I love to read challenging material.
3. I don't worry about things all the time.
4. I try to follow the rules.

Based on the answers test takers provided, Cattell then scored people on the sixteen traits. He elaborated on these traits in the following chart:

Trait	Low scorers tend to be more . . .	High scorers tend to be more . . .
Warmth	Aloof or detached	Outgoing or kindly
Reason	Concrete thinking or direct	Abstract thinking or imaginative
Emotional stability	Reactive or malleable	Stable or mature
Dominance	Cooperative or submissive	Assertive or competitive
Liveliness	Serious or prudent	Animated or spontaneous
Rule-consciousness	Expedient or self-indulgent	Dutiful or conscientious
Social boldness	Shy or timid	Venturesome or uninhibited
Sensitivity	Utilitarian or objective	Sentimental or refined
Vigilance	Trusting or accepting	Suspicious or skeptical
Abstractedness	Practical or conventional	Imaginative or impractical
Privateness	Genuine or open	Discreet or worldly
Apprehension	Self-assured or secure	Self-doubting or worried
Openness to change	Traditional or conservative	Experimental or critical
Self-reliance	Group-oriented	Solitary or resourceful
Perfectionism	Impulsive or uncontrolled	Organized or compulsive
Tenseness	Relaxed or patient	High energy or impatient

Cattell's 16PF questionnaire enjoyed considerable success around the world. The test was translated into more than thirty languages, and in the late twentieth century, many businesses and career counselors used it to evaluate job candidates and to match workers to jobs that called for traits resembling those displayed by the candidate.

Cattell's questionnaire fell out of favor in the 1980s, when other researchers began to criticize the methods he had used in creating the test. Other critics exposed statements made by Cattell that offered partial support for the eugenicist ideas of German dictator Adolf Hitler. During World War II, Hitler had arranged for the forced sterilization of hundreds of thousands of mentally disabled Europeans and had also had women impregnated in an effort to create a "master race" of blond-haired, blue-eyed Germans, whom he believed were superior to other people. Because of his support for Hitler's sinister experiments, Cattell lost respect in the psychological community.

THE EYSENCK PERSONALITY QUESTIONNAIRE

Psychologist Hans Eysenck, who worked in Great Britain, took a closer look at Cattell's sixteen traits. In 1957 he turned to advances in scientific technology—such as new methods of imaging the brain—along with refined factor analysis and intensive research into hundreds of personality tests, to reduce Cattell's sixteen traits to just two traits: extroversion and neuroticism.

Like earlier researchers, Eysenck defined extroversion as outgoingness and a desire to seek out and interact with others. He associated liveliness, excitability, sociability, and impulsiveness with this quality. He defined neuroticism as the tendency to suffer from negative emotions such as depression or anxiety. In 1975 Eysenck and his wife, Sybil, who was also a personality psychologist, added a third primary trait, which they called psychoticism. This trait describes a person's tendency to be aggressive or to be opposed to change. The Eysencks then devised a personality test, with questions such as those in the box on page 42, to analyze an individual's personality.

When Life throws You Lemons

Try the following experiment to determine your level of introversion or extroversion. It's based on Eysenck's research on personality traits.

You'll need these:

a length of thread sturdy enough to knot

a double-tipped cotton swab

an eyedropper or a toothpick

a small amount of lemon juice

Steps:

1. Tie the thread to the center of the swab. Make certain that it balances perfectly in the horizontal plane when allowed to dangle.
2. Swallow three times. Place one end of the swab in your mouth. Wait thirty seconds, using a watch, clock, or smartphone to measure the time.
3. Remove the swab. With an eyedropper or a toothpick, place four drops of lemon juice on your tongue. Swallow and then place the other end of the swab on your tongue in the spot where you dropped the lemon juice.
4. Wait another thirty seconds.
5. Pull out the swab. Take hold of the thread and allow the swab to dangle. Observe whether it balances horizontally or leans to one side or the other.

The Eysencks found that introverts produce more saliva in response to stimulants than do extroverts. Therefore, if your swab is not balancing horizontally, it probably means that excess saliva has made the lemon-juice side heavier: you're an introvert.

Why? Introverts, the researchers discovered, tend to be more physically sensitive than are extroverts. Their brains and bodies respond more to outside stimuli, such as noisy party conversation, jostling in crowds, loud music, and intense flavors. The strong stimulus of lemon juice causes more activity in an introvert's brain than in an extrovert's brain. This activity in turn causes the introvert to produce more saliva than the extrovert. Introverts also tend to sweat and fret more than extroverts.

TRY IT

1. Do other people think of you as being very lively?

2. Have you ever taken advantage of somebody?

3. Do you like socializing with people?

4. Does it worry you if you know there are mistakes in your work?

5. Have you ever felt listless and tired for no reason?

6. Do you not care if you are rude to people?

Take the boxed quiz above to see how you score in the Eysencks' personality model. Questions 1 and 3 measure extroversion. If you answered yes to these questions, you are likely more extroverted than introverted. If you answered no, the opposite is likely true. A yes answer to questions 4 and 5 indicate a tendency toward neuroticism. Those with high neuroticism scores tend to be anxious, moody, or unstable. Those with low neuroticism scores tend to be emotionally stable, calm, and unreactive. Questions 2 and 6 measure psychoticism. A yes answer to these questions suggests a more aggressive character. A no answer to both suggests a more empathetic character.

If you could not answer a firm yes or no to any of the above questions, that's actually typical. Not everyone strongly favors one end of a personality spectrum over the other. Eysenck himself acknowledged that more people were closer to the middle of each given spectrum than to either end. Imagine a scale between extroversion and introversion where 1 is wholly introverted and 10 is wholly extroverted. The vast majority of people will register as 4s, 5s, 6s, or 7s. Some may be 2s and 3s or 8s and 9s. Only a very few will be 1s or 10s. For almost any quality assessed in a trait-theory test applied to large groups of people, this distribution—with most people in the middle and fewer on the extremes—is the likely outcome.

FOUR

MODEL BEHAVIOR

During the 1920s, an American named Katharine Cook Briggs read Carl Jung's *Psychological Types* and grew fascinated with the concept of simplifying human communication and experience through personality profiling. In the years leading up to World War II, Briggs and her daughter, Isabel Myers, devised a personality test that came to be called the Myers-Briggs Type Indicator (MBTI).

The MBTI is based on the three main aspects of personality identified by Carl Jung: introverted versus extroverted, intuitive versus sensing, and feeling versus thinking. Briggs and Myers added a fourth aspect, judging versus perceiving, which concerns how much structure someone prefers. Myers and Briggs said that judges want things neatly organized and arranged in advance, and perceivers want flexibility.

Using a series of questions, the MBTI labels people on the four aspects. It assigns letters to the personality types, with *I* standing for introverted, *E* for extroverted, *N* for intuitive, *S* for sensing, *F* for feeling, *T* for thinking, *J* for judging, and *P* for perceiving. The four types can be combined in sixteen possible ways. So depending on test scores, a person is labeled either an INTJ, INFJ, ISFJ, ISTJ, INTP, INFP, ISFP, ISTP, ENTP, ENFP, ESFP, ESTP, ENTJ, ENFJ, ESFJ, or ESTJ. Each of these combinations reflects a specific personality type.

TWO WOMEN, TWO MILLION PEOPLE

Briggs and Myers were not trained psychologists. They created their test simply by surveying acquaintances and keeping track of their answers on thousands of note cards. They then attempted to show correlations between specific answers to questions and wider personality traits. After they ran out of acquaintances to survey, they had family and friends give questionnaires to their friends to collect more data.

Eventually, Briggs and Myers administered their test to college students: first at George Washington University Medical School in Washington, DC, and then at many colleges, nursing schools, high schools, and businesses around the United States. The test was said to produce dependably consistent results and quickly gained broad acceptance. In 1962 the Educational Testing Service, a company that develops and administers standardized tests, began distributing the MBTI to businesses, schools, and organizations interested in training, coaching, group dynamics, career development, and self-awareness. In 1975 Consulting Psychologists Press (CPP) bought the rights to publish the test. In the twenty-first century, people can obtain the test from CPP, both through its website (a self-assessment costs $49.95) and through counselors, psychologists, and others who enroll to become certified MBTI interpreters.

On a small scale, Briggs and Myers saw their assessment as an aid in the US war effort. During World War II, millions of American men left home to fight overseas. Women filled jobs in their absence. Briggs and Myers developed the test to help employers match a woman's self-defined qualities with a job that would suit her personality. Briggs and Myers also saw the assessment as a much broader tool to support communication among people of every nation, which they hoped would help end conflict and promote world peace.

Roughly two million people in about 170 countries take the MBTI every year, either on their own initiative, in counseling, or as part of workplace assessment. The Myers & Briggs Foundation explains that knowing another person's type provides a sort of crib sheet for effectively managing relationships. And by knowing your own type, you can become more aware of your habits, talents, and faults. This knowledge can help you make decisions, build on your strengths, and overcome your limitations.

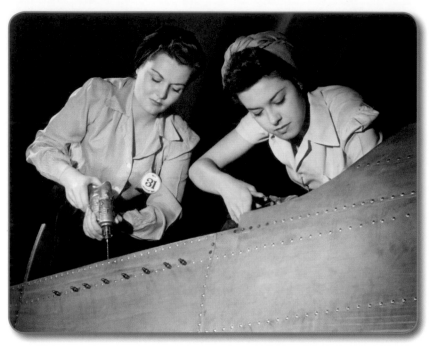

Katharine Cook Briggs and Isabel Myers believed that their type indicator would help match women with suitable jobs during World War II. During the war, many women worked in defense industries *(above),* filling jobs previously held by men. In modern times, employers still use the MBTI to match workers with appropriate jobs.

Unlike other personality models, whose primary traits have negative connotations (such as "low emotional stability"), the MBTI's sixteen personality types are expressed in positive language. The names emphasize that it is okay to be any one of sixteen types. Isabel Myers once made this point quite succinctly: "You psychologists focus on what is wrong with people; I want to focus on what is right and what could be right."

EVERYONE'S A CRITIC

The Myers-Briggs test has had detractors for decades. In 1993 David Pittenger, an assistant psychology professor at Marietta College in Ohio, published a critical analysis of the test. He noted that the MBTI measures personality factors as absolutes—that is, as black or white rather than in shades of gray. For each of the four aspects of personality, the MBTI assigns

a test taker a number. Anyone ranked between 1 and 5 in this system is considered a 1 (one extreme). Anyone who scores between 6 and 10 is considered a 10 (the other extreme). Pittenger challenged the test's claim that people are strongly attuned to one extreme or the other for any given trait. Using the 1 to 10 scale of extroversion as an example, Pittenger cited the MBTI's own data to show that the vast majority of people receive scores closer to the middle of each trait spectrum. But the test ignores this in favor of assigning people to the extremes.

Pittenger also criticized the reliability of the MBTI. One key criterion for measuring the effectiveness and legitimacy of any personality test is test-retest reliability. That is, the personality type results of any one test taker who takes the same test at different times must be consistent. Myers and Briggs claimed that an individual's MBTI type didn't significantly change over many decades. But studies have shown that when test takers take the MBTI once and then take it again five or more weeks later, 50 percent of them are classified as a different type on the second test.

Myers and Briggs also claimed that certain types were best suited to certain jobs. But Pittenger pointed to several studies that provided "no evidence to show a positive relation between MBTI type and success within

name of the game

Personality profiling has permeated the games we play. In the role-playing game Dungeons and Dragons, for instance, players take on the persona of characters who are categorized as lawful, neutral, or chaotic. Characters are also typed as either good or evil. The combination of types results in nine different alignments, or personalities. For example, the Crusader is a lawful and good character. The Rebel is a chaotic and good character. The Free Spirit is a chaotic and neutral character, and the Destroyer is a chaotic and evil character.

an occupation." In fact, the distribution of personality types in various professions simply reflects the distribution of personality types of the US population as a whole. For instance, in the MBTI model, 12 percent of elementary schoolteachers are ENTJs. This statistic might suggest that outgoing, intuitive people who think logically and work hard toward successful resolutions are well suited to jobs as schoolteachers. But Pittenger pointed out that ENTJs also comprise 12 percent of the general population. That means that ENTJs are no more likely to choose to become schoolteachers than any other MBTI type.

CPP, which publishes the MBTI along with about eight hundred other career coaching, training, and evaluation tools, refutes these criticisms. The company asserts that the test accurately measures everything it claims it does.

In the twenty-first century, many businesses still use the MBTI, but the professional psychological community has distanced itself from the test. Psychiatrists, psychologists, and researchers don't deny that the MBTI is popular and often useful, but they see the test as a self-help tool rather than as evidence-based science that has a proven record to effectively predict much of anything.

THE BIG FIVE

One of the most substantial advances in personality psychology since the late twentieth century has been the establishment of the Big-Five Factor Markers (BFFM). This is a list of five personality traits that the modern psychological community believes forms the core of all human personality. The five traits are openness to experience, conscientiousness, extroversion, agreeableness, and neuroticism. The acronym for these traits is OCEAN. The questions on the following page come from the BFFM test.

Since its creation in the 1980s, the BFFM test has been found to provide an accurate assessment of personality for people from more than fifty cultures worldwide, with a variety of languages and religious backgrounds. The BFFM has become the most widely used and trusted model of understanding personality. Psychologists, psychiatrists, and other health-care professionals use it to assess patients.

This is not to say that the assessment is flawless or exempt from criticism. One critique is that the BFFM model fails to successfully include every trait that can be considered important to an individual's personality. For example, the BFFM does not consider whether someone is moral or deceptive, masculine or feminine, witty or dry. Faultfinders say that this kind of omission casts doubt on the system as a whole.

TRY IT

How accurately do these statements describe you? Rate each statement with a number from 1 to 5. The number 1 means "not accurately at all" and 5 means "very accurately."

1. I am always prepared.
2. I have frequent mood swings.
3. I have a vivid imagination.
4. I sympathize with others' feelings.
5. I am the life of the party.

SCORING THE TEST

To understand your test results, think of statement 1 as it relates to conscientiousness: your level of organization and the care you take in carrying out your plans. The higher your rating on this statement, the more conscientious you are. Statement 2 relates to neuroticism. The higher your rating on this statement, the more likely you are to have low emotional stability. You might get angry, irritated, or upset easily. Statement 3 relates to openness, or your willingness to try to accept new things. The higher your rating on this statement, the more open you are to change. Statement 4 relates to agreeableness: your level of empathy or friendliness. The higher your rating on this statement, the more agreeable you are. Statement 5 relates to extroversion, or the extent of fulfillment from social interaction. The higher your rating here, the more likely you are to be outgoing.

finger-pointing

Using a ruler, measure the length of the index and ring fingers on your dominant hand (the hand you write with). Start at the bottom crease, where your finger meets your palm and measure to the end of the fingertip. Divide the length of your index finger by the length of your ring finger. This number is known as your 2D:4D digit ratio.

Some scientists who study gender, genetics, and the human body say that the relationship between your finger lengths might be connected to the amount of estrogen and testosterone (female and male hormones) to which you were exposed in your mother's womb. They believe that this exposure could have a bearing on your personality, such as how aggressive you are or whether you suffer from depression.

A Brazilian study from 2012 found that those with a lower ratio were less able to postpone gratification than those with a higher ratio. The researchers measured this ability by allowing preschoolers to choose to either eat one piece of candy right away or to wait twenty minutes and then eat two pieces. The study found that those with lower 2D:4D ratios were more likely to eat the candy right away—because they wanted immediate gratification. Another study found that women with high 2D:4D ratios are more likely to suffer from depression than those with low ratios.

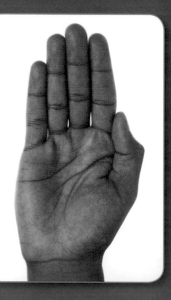

Scientists say that your exposure to male and female hormones before birth can affect your personality and can also affect the length of your fingers. Researchers have found that the 2D:4D ratio (the length of the index finger compared to the length of the ring finger) can be an indicator of aggression, friendliness, patience, and other traits.

A GEOMETRIC VIEW OF PERSONALITY: THE ENNEAGRAM

A popular personality typing system is called the enneagram. The nine-pointed symbol of the enneagram (from the ancient Greek words *ennea* for "nine" and *gramma* for "writing") has obscure origins. The ancient Greek philosopher and mathematician Pythagoras might have used the symbol to demonstrate mathematical relationships. The first person to connect the symbol to personality was twentieth-century Bolivian-born philosopher Oscar Ichazo, who employed it as part of a larger spiritual system. One of Ichazo's students, psychiatrist Claudio Naranjo, further developed the enneagram as a psychological tool in the early 1970s. In 1994 American Helen Palmer, a student of Naranjo's, founded the International Enneagram Association in Cincinnati, Ohio. Also in the 1990s, Americans Don Riso and Russ Hudson founded the Enneagram Institute in Stone Ridge, New York.

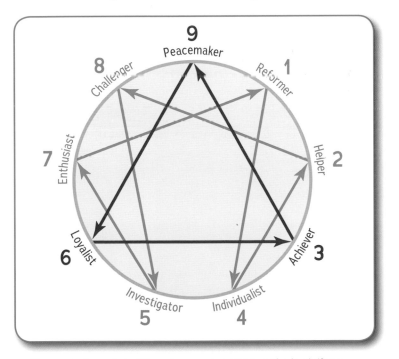

The ancient symbol of the enneagram serves as the basis for a popular personality typing system. The system divides people into nine different types.

The enneagram typing system helps people develop insight into themselves and others. Each of the nine points of the enneagram symbol represents one personality type. Some books and organizations, such as the Enneagram Institute (http://www.enneagraminstitute.com/), label the types with these names and numbers: Reformer (1), Helper (2), Achiever (3), Individualist (4), Investigator (5), Loyalist (6), Enthusiast (7), Challenger (8), and Peacemaker (9). Many adherents simply use the numbers 1 through 9 to name the types. You can take quizzes to figure out your enneagram type. But by far the most effective way to find your type is to read in-depth descriptions of the types in books or on websites. Then see which one best fits your sense of your own personality.

MORE NAYSAYERS

Many critics attack trait theory in general. They ask, Does it really help a person to discover a distinct number of identifiable personality behaviors? Does trait theory really help predict future behavior or help an individual better navigate the future? Many critics say no.

Critics point to another weakness with personality testing—the presumption that people will or can accurately describe themselves. Personality tests that rely on self-reporting gather information based on who test takers perceive themselves to be, which may not coincide with who they actually are. Just as we do not hear our own voices the way others hear them (listen to yourself on voice mail to hear this phenomenon), it is very easy to have misconceptions about your personality. You might think that you are more fun, stable, intellectual, social, crazy, logical, or impartial than you really are. And when taking a test, you might want to project an ideal self, a self you want others to find attractive, even if you know that what you're putting forth overlooks or exaggerates certain qualities.

Critics also say that trait theory is marked by oversimplification. Suppose a personality test told you that you were neurotic, or emotionally unstable. You wouldn't know if that meant that you were depressed or anxious— since many tests place these traits together. But the difference between depression and anxiety is significant. Classifying someone as generically neurotic is not meaningful, since it doesn't provide enough information to make useful decisions about a response or treatment plan, if necessary.

the heart of the Matter

Answer these questions based on your general behavior:

1. Do you enjoy completing projects?
2. Do you hate failure?
3. Do you prefer to stick with proven, time-tested methods as opposed to experimenting with new concepts or ways of doing things?
4. Do you describe yourself as unreflective?

If you answered yes to these questions, you might have what's called a type A personality. The type A label comes from cardiologists (heart doctors) Meyer Friedman and R. H. Rosenman. In the late 1950s, in their office in San Francisco, California, Friedman and Rosenman saw many patients who had been diagnosed with heart disease. Other patients who came to them for checkups or consultations turned out not to have heart disease. Observing patients in their waiting room, the doctors noted that some of them paced anxiously while others sat quietly. The doctors hypothesized that the patients who sat quietly handled stress better than those who paced and that they would be less likely to suffer from heart disease.

Friedman and Rosenman labeled the pacers type A. These people were focused on success. They did not like to take time off or slow down—viewing such behavior as slacking off. The doctors labeled the patients with calm personalities as type B. This group worked slowly and steadily toward their goals, without a fear of failing or falling behind.

To test their theory about stress and heart disease, Friedman and Rosenman conducted an eight-and-a-half-year study of healthy males between the ages of thirty-five and fifty-nine. The cardiologists concluded that those with type A personalities were more prone to have heart attacks than type Bs. Later studies disproved the doctors' theory, but the type A and type B labels persist in popular culture. That impatient person standing in line, the individual with a to-do list that just can't get done, that friend who's always interrupting and rushing—that's the quintessential type A.

Finally, critics say that trait theory ignores the context—the cultural framework we live in. For instance, what would it mean to say that a woman in nineteenth-century London—during an era when women were not allowed to vote, own property, or act independently of their husbands—was extroverted? Would she be similar to an extroverted London woman of the twenty-first century, an era in which women can vote, hold a wide range of jobs, and be elected to political office? Chances are, these two women would not have similar personalities. Throw into the mix such variables as money, education, religion, locale, health, family status, genetics, and social class, and it's impossible to say what a given trait as identified by a personality test actually expresses.

FIVE

Work, Play, Love

Many employers believe that gauging how a potential worker will perform in a job and helping employees better understand their own strengths and weaknesses can be a boon to productivity in the workplace. To this end, in 2014 an estimated 70 percent of US businesses used personality tests to evaluate potential and existing employees. That's double the number of businesses that used such tests in 2009. These numbers translate into hundreds of millions of dollars for companies that develop and sell personality tests, such as Hogan Assessment Systems and Evolv Inc.

Personality testing is a big business not only in the workplace. A broad range of schools, government agencies, and other groups incorporate tests into their training and communications programs. Courts sometimes use personality tests to determine which parent is better suited to take custody of children after a divorce. Some prisons use personality tests to determine whether a prisoner should be granted parole, or set free early. Schools sometimes use personality tests to diagnose kids with behavioral problems.

But personality testing has its brighter sides. In trying to match up romantic partners, dating websites such as eHarmony have customers take lengthy online personality tests. The websites use algorithms, or mathematical formulas, to analyze the test results and match test takers who might be romantically compatible. Galen Buckwalter, a psychologist

who created eHarmony's algorithm, explained, "We're not looking for clones, but our models emphasize similarities in personality and in values. It's fairly common that differences can initially be appealing, but they're not so cute after two years. If you have someone who's type A and real hard charging, put them with someone else like that. It's just much easier for people to relate if they don't have to negotiate all these differences."

TOP WORKPLACE TESTS

Many groups that employ personality testing use the MBTI or the enneagram. But a number of other tests are also popular. One is the Keirsey Temperament Sorter, created by psychologist David M. Keirsey and available for purchase from the company Keirsey.com. In his 1987 book *Portraits of Temperament*, Keirsey explained that his test was inspired by the old idea of the four humors. However, this test washes its hands of bodily fluids—blood, black bile, phlegm, and yellow bile—in favor of terms you can bring up at the dinner table or, since its typical users are members of a workplace, the conference table. The Keirsey test is a seventy-question multiple-choice quiz that divides test takers into four types you'll encounter at work: the Artisan, the Guardian, the Rationalist, and the Idealist.

Guardians are considered "concrete cooperators." They follow the rules, focus on duties, and respect and take care of others. Idealists are called "abstract cooperators." They act on what they hope for, believe in, and desire in good conscience. They are goal oriented, with a clear sense of ethics. Artisans are "concrete utilitarians." They get the job done, whatever it takes, even if that requires a little fudging of the rules.

US businesses spend millions of dollars per year on personality testing, but critics say that tests aren't very effective in predicting whether or not someone will succeed at a job.

They quickly and efficiently address immediate concerns. Rationalists are "abstract utilitarians." They're said to be practical. They're engaged by new problems and intrigued by possible solutions. They work toward goals pragmatically, which might involve sidestepping rules and conventions. Knowing your type, the test claims, will greatly improve your work performance.

For a quick personality assessment, some employers use the Color Code Personality Test, developed by psychologist and business coach Taylor Hartman. Test takers answer multiple-choice questions to determine which one of four colors—yellow, white, blue, or red—governs their personality. Those who test out to be governed by the color yellow are said to be optimistic. Whites are seen as calm and balanced. Blues are described as do-gooders. Reds are said to be leaders.

Another quick and easy assessment is the Psycho-Geometrics test. The test suggests that by picking one of the following five shapes, you will be making an unconscious projection of your personality:

TRY IT

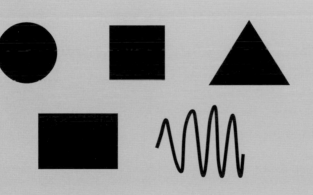

Yep, that's the gist of it. No secondary traits. No charts or list of questions. Corporate trainer Susan Dellinger designed the Psycho-Geometrics test in 1978. According to Dellinger, personality is based on the chosen shape, so circles are caretakers, triangles are ambitious, squiggles are free spirits who play by their own rules, squares value order and loyalty, and rectangles are adventurous.

Dellinger says that the Psycho-Geometrics test is just as valid as any other test on the market. But journalist Annie Murphy Paul criticizes that market as a whole. In her book *The Cult of Personality*, Paul writes,

> The reality is that personality tests cannot begin to capture the complex human beings we are. They cannot specify how we will act in particular roles or situations. They cannot predict how we will change over time. Many tests look for (and find) disease and dysfunction rather than health and strength. Many others fail to meet basic scientific standards of validity and reliability.

a better test

Developed at the University of Minnesota Hospital in 1937 by psychologists Starke R. Hathaway and J. Charnley McKinley, the Minnesota Multiphasic Personality Inventory (MMPI) is highly regarded in the field of mental heath. Psychiatrists and psychologists frequently use the MMPI to diagnose depression, paranoia, schizophrenia, and other disordered mental states in patients. Courts and law enforcement agencies often use the test to assess whether a criminal is mentally fit to stand trial.

Examiners know that some people who take tests try to present themselves in a favorable light—deliberately hiding their shortcomings or problem behaviors. They might give dishonest answers to test questions to try to slant an assessment. To protect against such false reporting, the MMPI includes a number of tools called validity scales. Examiners use these scales to determine whether MMPI test takers are answering truthfully or skewing results with dishonest answers. The scales point out inconsistencies, contradictions, and random answers that might indicate that a test taker is being deceptive.

SLEIGHT OF HAND

Yes, handwriting analysis is still alive and well. In the United Kingdom alone, more than three thousand companies use graphology tests to assess potential employees. Does handwriting analysis work? That question was put front and center in January 2005 when a group of British graphologists analyzed a sheet full of words and doodles created during a meeting of world leaders at the 2005 World Economic Forum. The doodles were attributed to Tony Blair, then prime minister of the United Kingdom. The graphologists agreed that these doodles were indicative of Blair's personality. According to the graphologists, Blair's circled words meant that he had a quick, flexible mind. The sloppy circles also showed that he had an inability to complete projects. His triangular doodles were said to represent a wish to get out of politics.

TRY IT

On a page of unlined paper, mark out a box the size of a postcard. With a pen, compose a sentence that includes your full name and occupies two or three lines.

Take a look at the sentence. Did you fill up your square completely, or did you leave a lot of white space? Handwriting analysts would say that the more empty space you left, the more withdrawn and shy you are. Similarly, is there a varying amount of distance between your written lines? That suggests less self-restraint and control than lines that are close together and more regularly spaced. If you drew a straight line under your words, do most of the letters rest on it? That indicates a more relaxed state of being. Flip over the page. Is your writing barely visible or indelibly incised into the paper? According to handwriting analysts, the pen's pressure indicates your level of energy: the deeper the groove, the greater the drive.

There was just one problem with the analysis of Blair's handwriting mentioned above: it turned out that Blair hadn't made the doodles after all. They were actually drawn by Microsoft founder Bill Gates, who had been at the same meeting. And the analysis of the doodles didn't fit Gates's life

"Sales dropped during the Depression" —but people to steal the candy for " supposed ability to resh time" —lots of sad songs written about people don their luck with no Wibbl to change their fate

Many companies, especially in the United Kingdom, use handwriting analysis to evaluate potential employees. Most scientists call the practice pseudoscience. They say that you can't learn anything about personality by analyzing someone's handwriting.

or situation at all. This example and others lead many, including the British Psychological Society, to say that graphology has no scientific basis. Despite its continued popularity, most experts call graphology a pseudoscience—or false science.

SCHOOL'S IN SESSION

Intelligence testing and skill testing are still common in the twenty-first century, in both schools and other settings. Businesses, researchers, government agencies, and the US military use tests such as the Wechsler Adult Intelligence Scale and the Stanford-Binet Intelligence Scale to assess a candidate's suitability for joining the team. The National Football League uses the Wonderlic Cognitive Ability Test, a twelve-minute, fifty-question exam, to determine players' aptitude for learning and solving problems. If you were a coach or a wide receiver, wouldn't you want to work with a quarterback who had tested well in the ability to retain strategies and to astutely problem-solve in unique situations?

Intelligence and skill tests have their drawbacks, however. Consider the SAT, previously called the Scholastic Aptitude Test and the Scholastic Assessment Test. Taken by most American high school students, the SAT is designed to test math and literacy skills that will be needed in college. But critics say that the SAT really measures only a test taker's aptitude for taking tests more than it assesses his or her skills. To some extent, it also measures a student's affluence. Students whose families can afford to send

them to expensive group or private SAT tutoring programs will generally score better than those who cannot afford the tutoring. Schools in wealthy neighborhoods—where many students are focused on being accepted to top colleges—are also more likely to incorporate testing preparation sessions into their curriculum than are those in poor neighborhoods. And most of this preparation boils down to test-taking practice, which has been shown to result in less anxiety at test time and better scores. In addition, critics say that many SAT test questions include vocabulary (such as *regatta*) and concepts that are more related to the concerns and experiences of upper-income students than to those of poor or middle-income students.

PHYSIOGNOMY FOR OUR TIMES

Experts in a variety of fields—including psychology, anatomy, evolutionary science, and genetics—call physiognomy a pseudoscience. They say it's impossible to judge someone's personality based on physical attributes. But even though physiognomy is long past its heyday, people still frequently judge others by aspects of their physical appearance. In what psychologists call the halo effect, we tend to assign positive qualities to those whom we perceive as physically attractive. For instance, people often equate handsomeness with honesty. They equate extreme good looks with morality, or goodness. Conversely, those the beholder finds less attractive are subjected to the horns effect. (Here the devil's horns are the reverse of the angel's halo.) They are subconsciously pigeonholed as less honest or less moral.

Edward Thorndike, an American educational psychologist, first coined the term *halo effect* in 1920. In a study with members of the US military, he had commanding officers rank soldiers in terms of their physique, as well as in terms of their leadership ability, intellect, and a range of personality traits. He found that an officer who rated a soldier's physique positively was more likely to give positive ratings to the soldiers' nonphysical attributes.

In later studies, people viewed photographs of faces and then speculated about whether those in the pictures were promiscuous or not, good or bad parents, happy or unhappy, successful and powerful in the workplace, and so on. Overwhelmingly, participants matched the more attractive faces with the

more positive qualities. In another study, from 1974, Michael G. Efran of the University of Toronto in Canada staged a series of simulated jury trials and found that the pretend jurors showed more leniency and awarded less severe punishments to attractive pretend defendants than to those who were not good looking.

The elements of physiognomy feed, consciously or unconsciously, into cultural assumptions. Who would you trust more: an unshaven, sloppily coiffed political candidate who slouches and stares at his feet or the one with upright posture, a radiant complexion, and eyes filled with youthful vigor? Most people would choose the better-groomed candidate.

Hollywood is very aware of this shorthand to personality assessment, and producers and directors take advantage of it. Consider characters in films and on TV. The sidekick is usually shorter and less attractive than the hero. The leading lady is frequently blond and beautiful. The villain is often dark complexioned and speaks with a foreign accent.

Some might argue that such profiling or stereotyping is a survival skill. Perhaps it's our animal nature to make snap decisions in an encounter: Is this person a threat or an ally? Yet it's just such snap decisions that create bigotry, hate crimes, job discrimination, and similar behaviors that plague society.

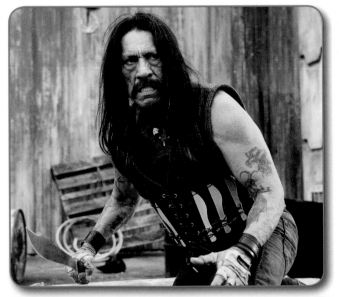

The halo effect and its opposite, the horns effect, frequently come into play in casting for Hollywood movies. The bad guy is frequently dark complexioned, unkempt, and unattractive. The hero is typically good looking.

SIX

Star power

many people, when asked about their personality type, refer to their zodiac sign. "Oh, I'm a typical Virgo." Or "I'm a textbook Scorpio." From a young age, Americans are surrounded by images of the zodiac, a chart showing the twelve astrological signs, each corresponding to a different period on the yearly calendar. If you were born between May 21 and June 21, for example, your sign is Gemini, and according to astrologers, you and other Geminis share certain personality traits.

Astrology has been around since ancient times, with variations in different parts of the world. In the West, astrology hasn't always been popular in the mainstream. That changed with the birth of Princess Margaret of the United Kingdom on August 21, 1930. Three days later, the *London Sunday Express* ran a full-page horoscope of the newborn princess, written by astrologer R. H. Naylor. The article predicted what the future would hold for Margaret. It created a massive surge of interest in astrology and prompted the newspaper to hire Naylor to write a weekly column.

Astrology can involve in-depth analysis. Astrologers look at the location of specific astral bodies and their position in certain houses, or portions of the sky, at a given time to come up with a picture of an individual's personality. But to keep things simple, Naylor focused principally on sun signs—the zodiac signs corresponding to where the sun was in the sky at the moment of a

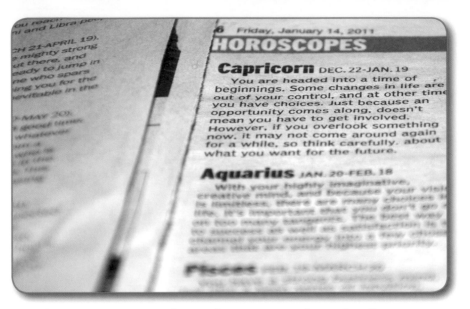

Horoscopes are common features in newspapers and magazines. Surveys have revealed that nearly one-third of Americans believe that horoscopes provide useful information.

person's birth. He then gave generalized advice and predictions for people born under each sign, claiming that the information came from his readings of the position of the stars and planets. Other newspapers followed suit, and by the twenty-first century, horoscopes were everywhere—in print publications and online.

SEEING STARS

A 2008 study showed that 31 percent of US citizens—approximately 94 million people—put some degree of faith in horoscopes. This number is 2 percent higher than for 2007 and 6 percent higher than for 2005. Astrology is popular well beyond the United States. An analysis of Google searches in English-speaking nations showed that people in India search for the word *astrology* the most, followed by people in South Africa, Singapore, Canada, and the United States. People frequently turn to astrology for advice and predictions about jobs and other daily activities. One of the most popular topics is romance. Astrologers frequently discuss which signs

of the zodiac are most romantically compatible and which zodiac matchups should be avoided. In parts of India, people turn to astrology to find suitable marriage partners.

Study after study has shown little or no statistically significant correlation between a person's zodiac sign and personality traits or occupation. But astrologers remain steadfast in their belief that they can read the stars, and millions of people put stock in astrological predictions. Why? There are several possible answers. First, most horoscopes provide positive messages. They give people hope that good things are coming—perhaps

new Moons

Chinese astrology has some similarities to Western astrology, but it is based on the Chinese lunar (moon) calendar instead of the Western solar (sun) calendar used in the United States. Each of the twelve signs of the Chinese zodiac corresponds to a year, which starts with the first new moon.

Individuals born during a certain year are said to share characteristics with a corresponding animal. For instance, if you're born in the Year of the Monkey, you'll be self-assured and innovative. If you're born in the Year of the Goat, you'll be shy and compassionate.

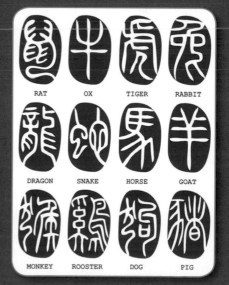

Horoscopes are popular worldwide. This chart shows the twelve signs of the Chinese zodiac with their accompanying Chinese characters.

with the new moon or the new year. In addition, some personality traits are difficult, if not impossible, to change. Rather than work hard to improve yourself, it's easier to say, "Yeah, I'm a Taurus. That's why I'm stubborn." In his book *Why Astrology Endures*, historian and social critic Theodore Roszak offers another reason for astrology's appeal. He writes, "The rich imagery of these old traditions has become a more inspirational way of talking [about ourselves] . . . than conventional psychiatry. The astrological universe is, after all, the universe of Greco-Roman myth, of [famous writers] Dante, Chaucer, Shakespeare, Milton, Blake. It has poetry and philosophy built into it."

Locate your birth year in this chart to see which animal guides your personality. (If your birth year isn't on the chart, remember that the cycle repeats every twelve years, so you can add more years to the chart, at either the top or the bottom, by adding or subtracting years and repeating the list of twelve animals.)

ANIMAL	TRAITS	BIRTHDAYS
Rabbit	Gentle, compassionate	2/16/1999–2/04/2000
Dragon	Intellectual, excitable	2/05/2000–1/23/2001
Snake	Wise, passionate	1/24/2001–2/11/2002
Horse	Zealous, generous	2/12/2002–1/31/2003
Goat	Polite, kind-hearted	2/01/2003–1/21/2004
Monkey	Innovative, versatile	1/22/2004–2/08/2005
Rooster	Ambitious, neat	2/09/2005–1/28/2006
Dog	Straightforward, courageous	1/29/2006–2/17/2007
Pig	Frank, calm	2/18/2007–2/06/2008
Rat	Adaptable, thoughtful	2/07/2008–1/25/2009
Ox	Industrious, respectful	1/26/2009– 2/13/2010
Tiger	Faithful, virtuous	2/14/2010–2/02/2011

WHY DO WE BELIEVE IT?

In 1948 psychologist Bertram R. Forer presented a personality test to his students. Then, deliberately ignoring their actual responses to the test, he assigned the same personality profile to each student. He then asked the students to evaluate their profiles on a scale from 1 to 5, according to how accurate they seemed to be. The class's ratings averaged a score of 4.25. That's an 85 percent acceptance rate. Stated differently, the vast majority of students accepted a profile of themselves that was not in any way based on their particular responses.

This anecdote demonstrates what has become known as the Barnum effect, based on wily showman P. T. Barnum's remark that his circuses had "something for everyone." The Barnum effect is the tendency of people to see special or personal meaning in uniform or general feedback, to feel that broad descriptions apply especially to them. In effect, people accept overly vague statements that are true for everyone (or nearly everyone) as being unique to their situations and as proof of the effectiveness of psychic readings, horoscopes, and personality tests. Some personality tests rely on the Barnum effect more than others.

POP! GOES THE POP CULTURE TEST

The Internet holds a remarkable variety of personality tests, developed by amateurs and available to those who know where to look or those who can't look away: try BuzzFeed, AllTheTests, Quizane, Quibblo, or Quizony. One of the most popular amateur tests on BuzzFeed is "What City Should You Actually Live In." It has logged more than twenty million views, and BuzzFeed offers hundreds of other tests.

In the digital age, online personality testing profiles rely primarily on word of mouth and social media sites such as Facebook for their success. Why do we take these tests? For one thing, most of them are free. And the most popular tests are those that tell people something about their interests and experiences. For instance, "dog people" like tests that tell them which breed of dog they are. "Cat people" enjoy tests that tell them which breed of cat they are (and, coincidentally, why they are better than dog people). Football fans choose tests that tell them which position they should play.

If the Shoe Fits

Try the Forer experiment yourself. Tell a few friends that with the aid of this book, you can create profiles of their personalities. Ask them some of the questions from the book or ask them to interpret inkblots, pick geometric shapes, or pick colors. Pretend to check the answers by thumbing through the back of the book. Then give them the following assessment (written by Forer):

> You have a need for other people to like and admire you, and yet you tend to be critical of yourself. While you have some personality weaknesses you are generally able to compensate for them. You have considerable unused capacity that you have not turned to your advantage. Disciplined and self-controlled on the outside, you tend to be worrisome and insecure on the inside. At times you have serious doubts as to whether you have made the right decision or done the right thing. You prefer a certain amount of change and variety and become dissatisfied when hemmed in by restrictions and limitations. You also pride yourself as an independent thinker; and do not accept others' statements without satisfactory proof. But you have found it unwise to be too frank in revealing yourself to others. At times you are extroverted, affable, and sociable, while at other times you are introverted, wary, and reserved. Some of your aspirations tend to be rather unrealistic.

Ask your friends how well this description fits. As long as you don't allow them to catch on that each person is being offered the same profile, chances are you'll find a high rate of acceptance. Most people will say that the profile fits.

Tests tell Marvel Comics fans which mutant power they have or which Avenger they are. Disney fans can learn via online tests which movie they should rewatch or which prince they should marry. *Avatar* fans can learn which element they can bend. Harry Potter fans can find out which house they should join.

Another attraction of these tests may be to improve communication. The digital age has made it easier to connect with more people more frequently. By mid-2015, Facebook had almost 1.5 billion monthly active users, and the average American had more than 300 friends. But it's hard to socialize, communicate, and keep in touch with so many "friends." Keith Wilcox, professor at Columbia Business School in New York, suggests that posting results from amateur tests on social media sites is one attempt to address this problem. He said, "I think it's tapping into a general trend on Social Media where Facebook has really become a platform for people to

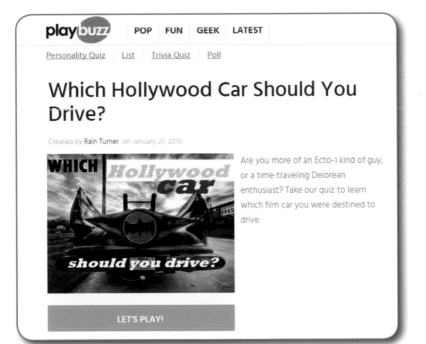

play buzz   POP   FUN   GEEK   LATEST

Personality Quiz | List | Trivia Quiz | Poll

Which Hollywood Car Should You Drive?

Created by Rain Turner on January 27, 2015

Are you more of an Ecto-1 kind of guy, or a time-traveling Delorean enthusiast? Take our quiz to learn which film car you were destined to drive.

LET'S PLAY!

Most people take online personality quizzes for a good laugh. The quizzes also help people connect with friends.

post positive things about themselves. . . . A BuzzFeed quiz is like a soft boast. It's a way for you to communicate how good you or your interests are without going overboard." So posting a test invites connection, which helps create community.

TEST TAKER BEWARE

Most people understand that tests found in magazines and online are usually not based in hard science and are mainly meant to inspire conversation, laughter, and camaraderie. Other kinds of personality assessments, such as the MMPI and BFFM, were developed with serious research based on scientifically sound data. Tests such as the MBTI and the enneagram—although less scientific—can also give people insight into their own behavior.

In the right hands, in the right context, personality tests can be effective and useful. But they can also be misused. Critics charge that workplace personality tests have been used to shut out job candidates with depression, bipolar disorder, and other mental health issues, in violation of state and federal laws. Annie Murphy Paul says that if an employer or school wants to give you a personality test, you should do your homework first. She suggests visiting the American Psychological Association web page at http://www.apa.org/science/programs/testing/rights.aspx. The page lays out "the Rights and Responsibilities of Test Takers." She also directs test takers to research tests online or at the library before agreeing to take them. Robyn Dawes, a psychologist at Carnegie Mellon University in Pittsburgh, Pennsylvania, encourages people to refuse testing if they feel that the results might lead to decisions with negative repercussions for their employment, schooling, health care, or family life. He especially warns against inkblots, sentence completion, and other projective tests, which he says are not valid. Paul adds, "If you go ahead with the test, inquire about how its results will be used, ask for feedback once it is scored, and request an assurance that your answers will be kept confidential."

Of course, if you're just looking for a quick laugh, there's no harm in taking online tests. Find a personality test that interests you and compare test results with your friends. This can be a great way to start a conversation and get to know more about one another. You may find that, yes, you're just my type!

source notes

5   Kay Ryan, *The Jam Jar Lifeboat and Other Novelties Exposed* (Kensington, CA: Red Berry, 2008), n.p.

9   Isabel Briggs Myers, "Quotes." MBTI-Coaching, accessed October 3, 2014, http://www .mbti-coaching.es/en/citas.html.

11   Lawrence A. Pervin and John P. Oliver, *Handbook of Personality: Theory and Research* (New York: Guilford, 1999), 4.

13   Claudius Ptolemy, *Tetrabiblos: Or the Quadripartite Mathematical Treatise*, trans. J. M. Ashmand (London: Davis and Dickson, 1822), 58, http://www.astrologiamedieval.com /tabelas/Tetrabiblos.pdf.

18   Thomas Browne, "Christian Morals, Part II," University of Chicago, accessed April 26, 2015, http://penelope.uchicago.edu/cmorals/cmorals2.html.

19   "The History of Phrenology on the Web," John van Wyhe, accessed April 26, 2015, http:// www.historyofphrenology.org.uk.

19   "Preface to: Familiar Lessons on Physiology," *Lost Museum*, accessed April 26, 2015, http:// chnm.gmu.edu/lostmuseum/lm/92/.

20   Sheila Lowe, *The Complete Idiot's Guide to Handwriting Analysis*. 2nd ed. (New York: Alpha: 2007), 6.

20   Shaike Landau, "Michon and the Birth of Scientific Graphology," British Institute of Graphologists, accessed April 20, 2015, http://www.britishgraphology.org/wp-content /uploads/2012/02/MichonAndTheBirthOfScientificGraphology.pdf.

20   "Cesare Lombroso," *New World Encyclopedia*, accessed April 26, 2015, http://www .newworldencyclopedia.org/entry/Cesare_Lombroso.

24   Scott Barry Kaufman, "Straight Talk about Twin Studies, Genes, and Parenting: What Makes Us Who We Are," *Psychology Today*, October 24, 2008, http://www.psychologytoday.com /blog/beautiful-minds/200810/straight-talk-about-twin-studies-genes-and-parenting-what -makes-us-who-w.

26   Sigmund Freud, *Dora: An Analysis of a Case of Hysteria*, ed. Philip Rieff (New York: Touchstone, 1997), 69.

29   Arthur S. Reber, *Penguin Dictionary of Psychology* (New York: Penguin, 1985), 653.

31   Shepherd Ivory Franz, "Handbook of Mental Examination Methods," Hathi Trust Digital Library, accessed May 29, 2015, http://babel.hathitrust.org/cgi/pt?id=mdp.39015026433907;view=1up;seq=183.

32   John B. Watson, *Behaviorism* (Chicago: University of Chicago Press, 1930), 82.

37   Annie Murphy Paul, *The Cult of Personality: How Personality Tests Are Leading Us to Miseducate Our Children, Mismanage Our Companies, and Misunderstand Ourselves* (New York: Free Press, 2004), 137.

39 Tim Flynn, "Cattell 16 Factor," *Similarminds.com*, accessed October 17, 2014, http://similarminds.com/cattell-16-factor.html.

42 Hans Eysenck and Sybil Eysenck. "Eysenck Personality Inventory," California, Educational and Industrial Testing Service, accessed August 26, 2014, http://legacy.library.ucsf.edu/tid/pfd3aa00.

45 Jason Rentfrow, "The Big 5 Model of Personality," *Psych Central*, accessed April 26, 2015, http://psychcentral.com/blog/archives/2009/11/10/the-big-5-model-of-personality/.

45 Jeanne Marlowe, "A Conversation with Katharine Myers on Myers-Briggs Personality Type and the MBTI Instrument," *Personality Pathways*, accessed October 3, 2014, http://www.personalitypathways.com/article/katharine-myers.html.

46–47 David Pittenger, "Measuring the MBTI . . . and Coming Up Short," *Journal of Career Planning and Placement* 20, no. 1 (Fall 1993), accessed August 27, 2014, http://www.fortunedotcom.files.wordpress.com/2013/05/mbti.pdf.

48 Graham Tyler, "Trait Theory, the Big-Five and the Five Factor Model," Asian Personality at Work Research Project, accessed August 26, 2014, http://www.personality.cn/personality_at_work_2.htm.

50 "Riso-Hudson Enneagram Type Indicator (RHETI) Sample," *9types.com*, accessed September 5, 2014, http://www.9types.com/rheti/index.php.

55 John Tierney, "Hitting It Off, Thanks to Algorithms of Love," *New York Times*, January 29, 2008, http://www.nytimes.com/2008/01/29/science/29tier.html.

56 David Keirsey, "Overview of the Four Temperaments," *Keirsey.com*, accessed August 28, 2014, http://www.keirsey.com/4temps/overview_temperaments.asp.

57 Paul, *Cult of Personality*, 221.

65 Theodore Roszak, *Why Astrology Endures* (San Francisco: Briggs, 1980), 8.

66 "Why Are We Hooked on Horoscopes," *Psychologies*, September 7, 2010, https://psychologies.co.uk/self/why-are-we-hooked-on-horoscopes.html.

67 "Forer Effect," *The Skeptic's Dictionary*, last modified September 12, 2014, http://skepdic.com/forer.html.

68–69 "Why Are BuzzFeed Quizzes So Popular? Experts Explain the Phenomenon," *Metro*, February 5, 2014, http://www.metro.us/news/why-are-buzzfeed-quizzes-so-popular-experts-explain-the-phenomenon/tmWnbe---47A1YyWNrLTY/.

69 Paul, *Cult of Personality*, 225.

glossary

A/B personality test: a test developed by cardiologists Meyer Friedman and R. H. Rosenman in the 1950s to determine whether aggressive and competitive people were more prone to heart disease than people who were more patient and calm. Although the doctors' theory about heart disease was shown to be incorrect, modern people still use the term *type A personality* to describe someone who is impatient and aggressive.

astrology: the study of how the sun, moon, planets, and stars relate to life, personality, and events on Earth. Astrology in the West has its roots in ancient Greece. Ancient Asian, Indian, and Middle Eastern cultures also developed systems of astrology.

Barnum effect: a tendency to accept overly vague or general statements that refer to one's own personality and characteristics even if they are technically inaccurate

Big-Five Factor Markers (BFFM): five personality traits that the modern psychological community believes form the core of all human personality. The five traits are openness to experience, conscientiousness, extroversion, agreeableness, and neuroticism.

enneagram: a personality typing system that includes nine types: Reformer, Helper, Achiever, Individualist, Investigator, Loyalist, Enthusiast, Challenger, and Peacemaker. People use the system to better understand themselves and how they relate to others.

eugenics: a movement that attempts to improve the human race by encouraging people with certain desirable traits to reproduce and discouraging others with less desirable traits from reproducing. In the twentieth century, eugenicists spearheaded the forced sterilization of thousands of mentally or physically disabled people, homosexuals, people of color, poor people, and other oppressed groups.

extrovert: a person who obtains fulfillment primarily from outside stimulation

graphology: the study of handwriting as a way of analyzing someone's personality

halo effect: the tendency of people to assign positive personality traits to good-looking people

heredity: the passing on of physical and mental characteristics from parents to their children through genetic material

horns effect: the tendency of people to assign negative personality traits to people who are considered unattractive

horoscope: a diagram or chart that shows the position of astral bodies at a certain time, such as the time of someone's birth. Astrologers use horoscopes to make assessments and predictions about people's lives and personalities.

humorology: the ancient Greek idea that the body contains four humors, or fluids, and that good health requires the balance of these fluids. Ancient doctors often tried to balance the humors by drawing blood from patients or by having them eat certain foods. In ancient Rome, Claudius Galenus expanded the concept of the four humors, connecting each humor to a personality type. The four humors are blood, yellow bile, black bile, and phlegm.

intelligence quotient (IQ): a number used to express the intelligence of a person, determined by a formula that compares the person's chronological age to his or her mental age, as determined by an intelligence test

introvert: a person who obtains fulfillment primarily from the world of one's own thoughts and interior life

mind-body dualism: the idea of French philosopher René Descartes in the seventeenth century that the mind and body operate together but that each entity has certain powers and certain limits

Minnesota Multiphasic Personality Inventory (MMPI): an extensive assessment tool used by doctors, law enforcement agencies, and others to diagnose people with depression, paranoia, schizophrenia, and other disordered mental states

Myers–Briggs Type Indicator: a widely used personality test that assesses whether people are introverted or extroverted, intuitive or sensing, feeling or thinking, and perceiving or judging. Many employers have used the system to better match workers with jobs.

nature versus nurture debate: the question, posed by early psychologists, of whether nature (inherited factors) or nurture (environmental surroundings) shapes personality. Most modern psychologists believe that personality is created by a combination of nature and nurture.

neuroscience: the study of the human brain and nervous system

personality: the set of behavioral, emotional, and intellectual characteristics that make each person unique

phrenology: the study of the shape of the skull, based on the false belief that its surface features are indicative of mental processes in the brain. German scientist Franz Josef Gall developed the study in the nineteenth century. The practice fell out of favor as scientists learned more about the brain in the late nineteenth century.

physiognomy: the practice of trying to discover someone's personality traits by looking at the person's outward appearance. Physiognomy has its roots in ancient Greece and ancient China. Although modern scientists say that it has no validity, studies show that people continue to judge others' personalities based on their looks.

projective test: a personality test that presents an object, word, or image to the test taker in an effort to stimulate a response that will expose the test taker's inner feelings. Rorschach inkblot and word association tests are examples of projective tests.

pseudoscience: a system of theories, assumptions, and methods that are not based on scientific methodologies

psychiatry: a branch of medicine that deals with mental, emotional, and behavioral disorders

psychoanalysis: a form of talk therapy through which patients examine their unconscious minds and bring their darkest secrets, ideas, and emotions to the forefront

psychology: the study of the human mind and behavior

Rorschach test: a projective test developed by Swiss psychiatrist Hermann Rorschach in the early twentieth century. The test consists of a series of inkblots presented on cards. Examiners look for patterns or themes that emerge in a test taker's responses to the images to try to learn about the test taker's behavior and personality.

test-retest reliability: a measure of whether a test is dependable based on multiple takings of the same test over time by the same person. A reliable test will give the same results each time it is taken.

Thematic Apperception Test (TAT): a projective test developed for the US Army in the 1930s. Test takers describe realistic scenes shown on a series of cards. Examiners analyze a test taker's descriptions and compare them to those provided by other test takers in an attempt to learn about a test taker's behavior and personality.

trait theory: a psychological approach to understanding human personality based on the idea that someone's personality is composed of unrelated but interacting patterns of behavior, thought, and emotion referred to as traits

unconscious: thoughts, ideas, and feelings that exist in people's minds without their conscious awareness. Sigmund Freud believed that unconscious motivations lie beneath the surface of our thoughts, projecting themselves—without our conscious permission or even our knowledge—onto our actions, reactions, and dreams.

selected bibliography

Baker, Kristin, Jean Graham, and Robert Lawson. *A History of Psychology: Globalization, Ideas, and Applications.* Uppler Saddle River, NJ: Pearson Prentice Hall, 2007.

Barenbaum, Nicole, and David Winter. *History of Modern Personality Theory and Research.* 3rd ed. New York: Guilford, 2008.

Borowka, Dana, and Ellen Borowka. "A Condensed History of Personality Tests at Work." Lighthouse Consulting, August 6, 2008. http://crackingthepersonalitycode.com/blog/2008/08 /condensed-history-of-personality-tests.html.

Cunningham, Lillian. "Myers-Briggs: Does It Pay to Know Your Type?" *Washington Post,* December 14, 2012. http://www.washingtonpost.com/national/on-leadership/myers-briggs-does-it-pay-to -know-your-type/2012/12/14/eaed51ae-3fcc-11e2-bca3-aadc9b7e29c5_story.html.

Frey, Rebecca. "Thematic Apperception Test." *Encyclopedia of Mental Disorders.* Accessed August 25, 2014. http://www.minddisorders.com/Py-Z/Thematic-Apperception-Test.html.

Grandoni, Dino. "Mastermind behind BuzzFeed's Quizzes Explains How They Work and Why They're So Crazy Viral." *Huffington Post.* Last modified February 24, 2014. http://www.huffingtonpost .com/2014/02/20/buzzfeed-quiz-how-do-they-work_n_4810992.html.

Gregory, Robert. *Psychological Testing: History, Principles, and Applications.* 4th ed. Cranbury, NJ: Pearson, 2004.

Lilienfeld, Scott. "Projective Measures of Personality and Psychopathology: How Well Do They Work?" *Skeptical Inquirer* 23, no. 5 (1999): 32–39. http://www.appstate.edu/~bromanfulksj /Lilienfeld%20-%20Projective%20Measures%20of%20Personality.pdf.

McAdams, Dan. "The Five Factor Model in Personality: A Critical Appraisal." *Journal of Personality* 60, no. 2 (1992): 329–361.

McCrae, Robert, and Oliver John. "An Introduction to the Five-Factor Model and Its Applications." *Journal of Personality Impact Factor* 2, no. 44 (1991): 175–215. http://www.workplacebullying .org/multi/pdf/5factor-theory.pdf.

Paunonen, Sampo, and Douglas Jackson. "What Is Beyond the Big Five? Plenty!" *Journal of Personality* 68, no. 5 (2000): 821–835. http://www.subjectpool.com/ed_teach/y4person/1_intro/refs /whatsbeyondthebig-5.pdf.

Pittenger, David. "Measuring the MBTI . . . and Coming Up Short." *Journal of Career Planning and Placement* 20, no. 1 (Fall 1993). Accessed August 27, 2014. http://www.fortunedotcom.files .wordpress.com/2013/05/mbti.pdf.

Roller, Emma. "Which Type of Internet User Are You?" *Slate,* January 29, 2014. http://www.slate.com /articles/life/culturebox/2014/01/buzzfeed_quizzes_taking_over_facebook_feeds_what_makes_ them_so_shareable.html.

Tyler, Graham. "Trait Theory, the Big-Five and the Five Factor Model." Asian Personality at Work Research Project. Accessed August 26, 2014. http://www.personality.cn/personality_at_ work_2.htm.

for further information

Books

Benson, Nigel. *The Psychology Book: Big Ideas Simply Explained.* New York: DK, 2012.

Burnham, John, ed. *After Freud Left: A Century of Psychoanalysis in America.* Chicago: University of Chicago Press, 2014.

Cain, Susan. *Quiet: The Power of Introverts in a World That Can't Stop Talking.* New York: Broadway, 2013.

Daempfle, Peter. *Good Science, Bad Science, Pseudoscience, and Just Plain Bunk: How to Tell the Difference.* Lanham, MD: Rowman & Littlefield, 2012.

Dunne, Claire. *Carl Jung: Wounded Healer of the Soul.* London: Watkins, 2012.

Kaye, Megan. *Do You Know Who You Are? Discover the Real You.* New York: DK, 2014.

Nettle, Daniel. *Personality: What Makes You the Way You Are.* New York: Oxford University Press, 2009.

Paul, Annie Murphy. *The Cult of Personality: How Personality Tests Are Leading Us to Miseducate Our Children, Mismanage Our Companies, and Misunderstand Ourselves.* New York: Free Press, 2004.

Rosen, Michael J. *Girls vs. Guys: Surprising Differences between the Sexes.* Minneapolis: Twenty-First Century Books, 2015.

Time. *The Science of You: The Factors That Shape Your Personality.* New York: Time, 2013.

Tomlinson, Stephen. *Head Masters: Phrenology, Secular Education, and Nineteenth-Century Social Thought.* Tuscaloosa: University of Alabama Press, 2013.

Weeks, Marcus. *Heads Up Psychology.* New York: DK, 2014.

Wittenstein, Vicki Oransky. *For the Good of Mankind? The Shameful History of Human Medical Experimentation.* Minneapolis: Twenty-First Century Books, 2014.

Websites

British Institute of Graphologists
http://www.britishgraphology.org/
The practice of handwriting analysis is especially popular in Great Britain. This website from the British Institute of Graphologists discusses the history of graphology and how it is used in the modern world.

Cracking the Personality Code
http://crackingthepersonalitycode.com/blog/
This site offers articles on the history and practice of personality testing.

Enneagram Institute

http://www.enneagraminstitute.com/

Created by Don Riso and Russ Hudson, the Enneagram Institute offers training and information on the use of the enneagram to understand personality. The website offers online personality tests, information on the nine enneagram types, FAQs, and additional resources.

The Jung Page

http://www.cgjungpage.org/

This website is dedicated to the work and life of Swiss psychiatrist and psychotherapist Carl Jung. This site includes information on Jung's work on personality typing as well as information about trait theory and the Myers-Briggs Type Indicator.

Myers & Briggs Foundation

http://www.myersbriggs.org/

The Myers & Briggs Foundation website is a vast source of information on the Myers-Briggs Type Indicator. The site describes the sixteen different MBTI types, how they interact, and how to use MBTI information in personal and professional environments.

Rights and Responsibilities of Test Takers: Guidelines and Expectations

http://www.apa.org/science/programs/testing/rights.aspx

Created by the American Psychological Association, this web page lists the rights of those who undergo psychological testing. These include the right to be treated with courtesy and respect, to be tested with measures that meet professional standards, to be provided with an explanation of the purposes for testing, and to be told of any consequences of taking or not taking the test. The page also lists a test taker's responsibilities, such as the responsibility to answer test questions honestly.

Sigmund Freud—Online Resources

http://www.freudfile.org/resources.html

Sigmund Freud's name is synonymous with psychology and psychoanalysis. This website offers a timeline of Freud's accomplishments, links to his written works, a glossary of Freudian terms, and more.

Similar Minds

http://similarminds.com

This website offers a large collection of personality tests, including free versions of many tests mentioned in this book.

Skeptic's Dictionary

http://skepdic.com/

This site examines pseudoscience, paranormal and supernatural beliefs, and other ideas and practices that are not backed up by science. It explains why people are drawn to such ideas and includes information on pseudosciences such as astrology, graphology, and phrenology.

index

Adler, Alfred, 27
aggression, 49
animals and human personality types, 17, 18, 32, 34, 64–65
anxiety, 27, 31, 40, 51, 60
Aristotle, 20
astrology, 12–14, 62–65
    Chinese horoscopes, 64–65
    popularity of, 63
    zodiac signs, 62, 64
attractiveness, 60–61
    halo effect, 60–61
    horns effect, 60–61
    See also physiognomy

Barnum effect, 66
behaviorism, 31–33
    reward and punishment, 32
Big-Five Factor Markers (BFFM), 47–48
body fluids
    See humorology
brain, 7, 8, 9, 18–19, 21, 22, 26, 29, 40, 41
    limbic system, 7, 9
    neurotransmitters, 8
Briggs, Katharine Cook, 43–45
Browne, Thomas, 18

Cattell, Raymond, 38–40
    Sixteen Personality Factor (16PF) questionnaire, 39
children, 24–25, 35, 54
China, 13, 17, 20
civil service test, Chinese, 16
criminology, 20–21, 28, 35, 54, 57
criticisms of personality tests, 10, 28–29, 33, 40,
    45–47, 48, 51, 53, 57, 58–61, 64–65, 69
culture, influence of, 13, 30–31, 34–35, 53

dating websites, 11, 54–55
    eHarmony, 54–55
delayed gratification
    See patience
depression, 40, 49, 51, 57, 69
Descartes, René, 22, 23, 26
diagrams, 9, 19, 50
doctors, 7–8, 14–15, 18, 22, 26–27, 52
dreams, 26–27
Dungeons and Dragons, 46

emotions, 9, 15, 20, 26–27, 40
employment, tests used in, 10, 16, 40, 44, 45, 46–47, 63, 69
enneagram, 50–51, 55, 69

eugenics, 35
    and Adolf Hitler, 40
extroversion and introversion, tests to measure, 40, 41, 42, 47–48
Eysenck, Hans, 40–42

Facebook, 66, 68–69
fears, 26–27, 28, 31, 32, 52
finger length
    hormones and, 49
    and personality, 49
food and diet, 15, 26
food preferences, 7
forecasting the future, 13, 51, 62, 64–65
Forer experiment, 66, 67
four humors, 14–15, 55
Fowler, Lydia, 19
Freud, Sigmund, 26–27

Galenus, Claudius (Galen), 15
Gall, Franz Josef, 18–19
gender (sex), 49
graphology, 20, 58–59

halo effect, 60–61
health, 14–15
    mental health, 30–31, 33, 40, 49, 51, 57, 69
heart disease and stress, 52
heredity, 24–25
Hippocrates, 14–15
Hirsch, Alan, 7
history
    China, 13, 16, 17, 20
    Greece, 14–15, 17, 20
    Iraq (Babylon), 12–13
    Middle Ages, 18
    Rome, 15
homosexuality, 10
horns effect, 60–61
human behavior, study of, 8–10, 20–21, 22, 24–25,
    26–27, 28–29, 32–33, 36–37, 51, 52, 54, 57, 69
humanism, 33
humorology, 14–15

income and test scores, 59–60
intelligence quotient (IQ), 33–35
intelligence tests, 16, 33–35
    Binet-Simon Intelligence Scale, 33
    SAT (Scholastic Aptitude Test), 59–60
    Stanford-Binet Intelligence Scale, 35, 59
    Wonderlic Cognitive Ability Test, 59
Iraq (Babylon), 12–13

Jung, Carl, 27, 36–37, 43

memory, 26
mental health, 30–31, 33, 40, 49, 51, 57, 69
Michon, Jean-Hippolyte, 20
mind-body dualism, 22, 23
Minnesota Multiphasic Personality Inventory (MMPI), 57
Minnesota Twin Family Study, 24
Myers, Isabel, 9, 43, 45
Myers-Briggs Type Indicator (MBTI), 9, 43–47
    criticism of, 45–47
    psychological types, 43

nature versus nurture, 23, 24–25, 38
neuroscientists, 7, 8
neuroticism, 40, 42, 47, 48

patience, 38, 49
personality, definition of, 8–9
personality tests, 9–11, 31, 40, 66
    amateur, 10–11
    business of, 10, 54
    criticism of, 40, 45–47, 48, 51, 53
    history of, 8–11
    misuse of, 10, 69
    online, 11, 54–55, 66, 68–69
    reliability of, 51, 57
    uses of, 10–11, 16, 20–21, 27–35, 40, 44–45,
        46–47, 54–56, 61, 63, 69
personality tests, types of
    A/B type test, 52, 55
    Big-Five Factor Markers (BFFM) test, 47–48
    Color Code Personality Test, 56
    enneagram, 50, 51, 55, 69
    Eysenck Personality Questionnaire, 40–42
    Forer experiment, 67
    Keirsey Temperament Sorter, 55–56
    Minnesota Multiphasic Personality Inventory
        (MMPI), 57
    Psycho-Geometric test, 56–57
    Rorschach test, 28–29, 30
    Sixteen Personality Factor (16PF) questionnaire,
        39
    Thematic Apperception Test (TAT), 29–31
    Woodworth Personal Data Sheet, 31
    word association tests, 27–28
phrenology, 18–19

physical appearance, halo and horns effects, 60–61
    See also physiognomy
physiognomy, 17–18, 20–21, 60–61
pseudoscience, 9, 29, 59, 60
psychiatry, 8, 10, 27–29, 37, 47, 50, 57, 65
psychoanalysis, 26–27
psychology, 8, 10, 24, 27, 29, 31–32, 33, 34, 36, 37–38,
    40, 44, 47, 54–55, 56, 57, 60, 66, 69
psychoticism, 40, 42
Ptolemy, Claudius, 13–14
Pythagoras, 50

racial profiling, 21
"Rights and Responsibilities of Test Takers," 69
Rorschach test, 28–29, 30

saliva test for introversion, 41
schizophrenia, 28, 57
self-help, 47
sexuality, 10, 26, 28, 35
skull shape, study of
    See phrenology
social media, 66, 68–69
stereotypes, 61
stress, 31, 38, 52

talk therapy
    See psychoanalysis
technology
    electroencephalograph (EEG), 8
    positron emission tomography (PET), 8
test-retest reliability, 46
trait theory, 36–42
Try It activities, 14, 27, 31, 38, 42, 48, 56, 58
twin studies, 24–25
type A and B personalities, 52, 55

unconscious mind, 8, 20, 26 28, 31–32, 37
US military, 29–31, 34, 60–61

Watson, John B., 31–33
Woodworth Personal Data Sheet, 31
workplace, personality tests in, 9–10, 16, 40, 44, 45,
    46–47, 63, 69
World War I, 31, 34–35
World War II, 20–21, 30, 40, 43, 44, 45

zodiac signs
    See astrology

photo acknowledgments

The images in this book are used with the permission of: © iStockphoto.com/dan4, (people backgrounds); © iStockphoto.com/Greeek (geometric backgrounds); © iStockphoto.com/Photolyric, p. 7; © Laura Westlund/Independent Picture Service, pp. 9, 51, 56; © Universal History Archive/ UIG/Bridgeman Images, p. 12; The Granger Collection, New York, p. 15; Courtesy of the National Library of Medicine, p. 18; © Charles Walker/Topfoto/The Image Works, p. 19; © Illustration from 'De Homine Figuris' by Rene Descartes (1596-1650) published in The Hague, 1662 (engraving), French School, (17th century)/Bibliotheque de l'Institut de France, Paris, France/Archives Charmet / Bridgeman Images/Bridgeman Images, p. 23; © Image Source/Getty Images, p. 25; © Time Life Pictures/Mansell/The LIFE Picture Collection/Getty Images, p. 26; © spxChrome/E+/Getty Images, p. 29; © Universal History Archive/Getty Images, p. 34; © CORBIS, p. 37; © George Marks/Retrofile Creative/Getty Images, p. 45; © Thomas Northcut/Photodisc/Getty Images, p. 49; © iStockphoto. com/Studio-Annika, p. 55; © Todd Strand/Independent Picture Service, p. 59; Twentieth Century Fox/The Kobal Collection/T/Art Resource, NY, p. 61; © EVA HAMBACH/AFP/Getty Images, p. 63; © kmt_rf/Alamy, p. 64; via Playbuzz, p. 68.

Front cover: © iStockphoto.com/dan4.

about the author

Michael J. Rosen is the author of more than one hundred books for readers of all ages, including nonfiction, humor, poetry, young adult novels, anthologies, and picture books. Recent nonfiction titles for young adult readers include *Place Hacking: Venturing Off Limits, and Girls vs. Guys: Surprising Differences between the Sexes.* He lives in the foothills of the Appalachians in central Ohio. His website is www.fidosopher.com.

Daniel Carlson is a graduate of Denison University in Ohio. In addition to collaborating on *Just My Type*, he worked with Michael J. Rosen on *Place Hacking: Venturing Off Limits.*

Contents

INTRODUCTION
me, myself, and i 6

One
Original thinking 12

two
mind and matter 22

three
trait theory. 36

four
model behavior 43

five
Work, play, Love 54

six
star power 62

Source Notes 70
Glossary 72
Selected Bibliography 74
For Further Information 75
Index 77

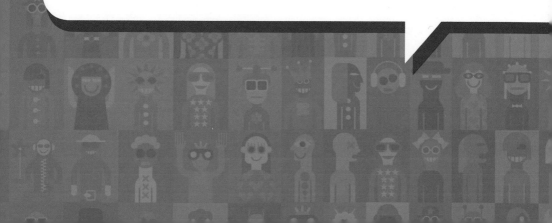